THE
LITTLE
BOOK
OF THE
EAST END

DEE GORDON

First published 2010

The History Press
The Mill, Brimscombe Port
Stroud, Gloucestershire, GL5 2QG
www.thehistorypress.co.uk

British Library Cataloguing in Publication Data.
A catalogue record for this book is available from the British Library.

ISBN 978 0 7524 5717 8

Typesetting and origination by The History Press
Printed in Great Britain
Manufacturing managed by Jellyfish Print Solutions Ltd

CONTENTS

INTRODUCTION

As an East Ender myself, I know that the description 'East End' means different things to different people. So, for the record, 'my' East End is bordered by Aldgate in the west, the River Lea in the east, the River Thames in the south, and Hackney Road in the north. So Spitalfields, Shoreditch, Poplar and East Smithfield, for example, are in the East End, but Hackney, Walthamstow, West Smithfield, Stratford and Dalston are not.

There follows an amalgam of fascinating facts that will interest the trivia buff, the historian, East Enders (past and present), tourists and just the downright curious. Whether you want to learn, to smile, or to be amazed . . . then there's something here for you. Here's a small taster of what's in store:

When Poplar became a parish in the early nineteenth century, they had to provide their own fire engines. By 1819, they had the ladder – but the fire engine didn't arrive for another four years.

The earliest person known to have lived in London was found in Blackwall, in the Yabsley Street area. The skeleton found here, in a crushed burial (indicating, by its foetal position, either a ritualistic return to Mother Earth, or, more practically, the need for a much smaller grave) was dated back to the Neolithic period, around 4,000 BCE.

When slavery was abolished in the nineteenth century, most of the 15,000 (*circa*) Londoners who were freed were living in the East End (London being the fourth largest slaving port in the world).

The first Peabody Buildings (housing for those on the lowest of low incomes) were built in Commercial Street, Spitalfields, in 1864. The tenants were provided with the luxury of nearby shops, baths and laundries, and the buildings remain, but as private housing.

The designer of St Patrick's Cathedral in Melbourne was William Wardell from Cotton Street, Poplar, the son of a baker who was Master of the Poplar Union Workhouse. He emigrated to Australia in 1858, the year the work was commissioned.

There were more Irish in the East End than in Dublin following the Irish famine of the 1840s.

In February 1756, Mary Jenkins, who sold old clothes at the Rag Fair in Rosemary Lane, sold a pair of breeches for 7*d* and a pint of beer. The breeches turned out to be worth rather more, however, when the purchaser ripped open the waistband and discovered eleven gold Queen Anne guineas and a £30 banknote.

Officially, no Cockneys were born between 11 May 1941 and 21 December 1961 because Bow Bells (in the City of London) were destroyed in an air raid and not restored for twenty years.

In 1911, Thomas Cook featured an 'Evening Drive in the East End' for 5*s*, in their brochure *How to See London*. These ran every weekday from Ludgate Circus to Whitechapel, Bethnal Green, Limehouse and China Town. Their programme was particularly reassuring that this 'unique evening drive incur no personal danger' with only one stop – at the People's Palace – where passengers would alight. They also stressed the area's 'good policing' with the 'sweeping away of many vile alleys' in spite of the 'almost entirely unrelieved sordidness' – it must have been a charming way to spend an evening!

The Lansbury Estate in Poplar was built as part of the 1951 Festival of Britain to provide an example of futuristic housing in an exhibition of live architecture. The strap-line was 'New Homes Rise from London's Ruins'. However, the transport links between it and the Festival Hall on London's South Bank had not been effectively planned, and far less people than anticipated made the trip to the East End to view the new estate.

The first beauty competition to be held in the East End was at the Cambridge Music Hall, Spitalfields, in 1904. Entrants were not allowed to wear make-up, and the competition was won by the natural beauty of Miss Rose Joseph.

CRIME & PUNISHMENT

PUNISHMENTS IN THE GOOD OLD DAYS

Gallows

Until the fifteenth century, pirates were often hanged on a gallows raised on a hill by East Smithfield, but the scaffold was then moved to Wapping where it became known as Execution Dock (on the site of what is now Wapping Underground). Famous executions that took place here included that of Captain William Kidd, hanged in 1701 (a pub named after him remains in Wapping High Street). The last men to be hanged for murder and mutiny on the High Seas were George Davis and William Watts, hanged here in December 1830. The gibbet was constructed low enough to the water so that the bodies could be left dangling until they had been submerged three times by the tide. On a 1746 map of the Isle of Dogs, other gibbets were indicated on the riverside.

Stocks

One (of many) remains in the vestibule of St Leonard's Church, Shoreditch, along with the parish whipping post.

Pillories

Some locations (again of many) were at Red Lion Street in Whitechapel, Broad Bridge in Ratcliff, Broad Street in Wapping, the village green at Bromley-by-Bow and opposite Christ Church, Spitalfields.

Other Methods of Chastisement

A ducking pond stood on Whitechapel Green for ducking scolds, drunks, gossips and witches.

A prison and court house were established in Neptune Street (the South side of Wellclose Square) by the eighteenth century, originally for debtors but extending its brief later. One plea, dated 1758, reads 'Please to remember the poor debtors'. Although there are stories of it being linked by tunnel to the Tower of London and the docks (from which the convict ship *Success* left), this seems unlikely. A part of a cell from this prison can be seen in the Museum of London, complete with graffiti of such images as a hangman, seemingly etched with a pine cone.

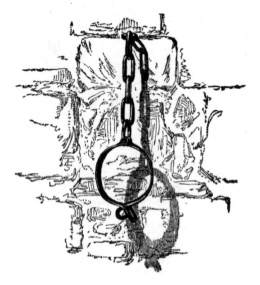

There are also records of an eighteenth-century prison specifically for debtors (known as Whitechapel Prison), alongside a 'court of record' for debts of under £5 'contracted in Stepney', which was located in Whitechapel Road.

The guard house which remains on the Isle of Dogs had a twin, both next to a drawbridge over the moat around the dock walls (from 1803), which was used for holding prisoners in the short term (the other was an armoury but is now a newsagent!).

Poplar Gaol, incidentally, was not what it seems – it was the name given to Poplar Baths when they opened in 1934 in East India Dock Road, thanks to its grim exterior.

GRIM GANGLAND DAYS

Notorious gangs in the East End over the years include:
Unemployed gangs of casual labourers who specialised in ambushing droves of cattle on their way to Spitalfields Market, covering the area between Stratford and Old Ford in the nineteenth century.

The Old Nichol Gang, who were responsible for terrorising local residents in Shoreditch in the nineteenth century.

The same period also boasted the Monkey Parade along Bow Road – gangs of teenage boys who molested passers-by, using lamp black to smear their faces, undeterred by fines of up to 10s.

A little later came the Bessarabian Tigers, mainly from the Bessarabia region of Romania, who specialised in blackmailing prospective brides with skeletons in their particular closet as well as running a pre-Krays protection racket. They were also known as the 'Stop at Nothing Mob' and wore distinctive oversized jackets and peacock feathers.

The Odessans from the Odessa café in Stepney, one that refused to pay protection, became a gang with a similarly violent reputation.

Bogard's Coons supplied muscle for street traders, and were led by Ikey Bogard, a Jewish pimp who dressed as a cowboy.

The Watney Streeters, probably the largest gang, had one particular member – George Cornell – who was unlucky enough to clash with the Krays.

The Sabini Brothers – six of them – came from Hoxton. They were known as 'The Italian Mob' and were said to import 'assistance' in the form of extra gangsters from Sicily, and specialised in race course crime after the First World War.

The Vendetta Mob, run by Arthur Harding from the slums of 'The Nichol' in Bethnal Green, had a preference for holding up card games in the Jewish 'spielers' (gambling houses) and claiming the proceeds – often just a few pounds.

P.S. The 2002 video game *The Getaway* features the Bethnal Green Mob, an 'old style' family of Cockney criminals.

TWENTY JACK THE RIPPER SUSPECTS

Prince 'Eddy' Albert Victor, Duke of Clarence, said to have fathered an illegitimate child following his visits to brothels. His hunting experience would have provided knowledge regarding disembowelling, and his activity could have been prompted by a possible diagnosis of syphilis, adversely affecting his decisions and behaviour.

James Stephen, the Duke of Clarence's tutor at Cambridge, who was gay and quite possibly jealous of the duke's heterosexual relationships. This gives two potential reasons for murder: a cover up for the duke, or jealousy. He allegedly starved himself to death (sources vary) after the duke died.

Sir William Gull, Physician-in-Ordinary to Queen Victoria and freemason, reported to have been seen in the area at the right time, also with a reason for covering up scandal.

John Maybrick, who was murdered by his wife in 1889. His diaries turned up in 1992 'revealing' (contentiously) his identity as Jack the Ripper.

Irishman Dr Francis Tumblety who fled London at the right time (1888) while awaiting trial for indecent assault – he died in 1903 leaving a collection of preserved uteruses behind.

Dr Grant, or Michael Ostrogg, who may have been a ship's surgeon but was certainly a confidence trickster. He spent several spells in asylums.

Frederick Deeming, who murdered his children and two wives, the second in Australia, for which he was hanged in 1892.

John or Jack Pizer, known as Leather Apron, a Jewish shoemaker with a collection of lethal blades. He had a conviction for stabbing and fitted the available description(s).

Aaron Kosminski was a Polish-Jewish hairdresser with mental health issues who lived with his two sisters in Sion Square, off Whitechapel Road. He was committed to an asylum in 1890, and said to 'hate' prostitutes. He survived another twenty-eight years.

Dr Thomas Cream, a specialist in carrying out abortions, who was subsequently hanged for poisoning some of his patients both in America and in South London. He is said to have confessed on the gallows.

Carl Feigenbaum, who faced the electric chair for murdering a woman in New York, was named by his lawyer (!) as Jack the Ripper after his client's death.

William Bury who was hanged for the murder of his prostitute wife in April 1889, her body mutilated in similar fashion to the Ripper's victims.

Walter Sickert, the artist, who may have been responsible for the anonymous confessional (?) letters sent to the police, and took a detailed interest in the murders.

Sir John Williams, royal obstetrician, said to have killed the prostitutes to research infertility.

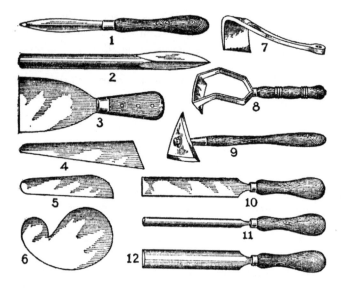

Montague Druitt, whose father, uncle and cousin were all doctors. He was often in the area visiting his mother in a Whitechapel asylum, and he was found drowned in the Thames in December 1888, perhaps having committed suicide after the murders.

Joseph Barnett, the lover of the Ripper's last victim, Mary Kelly. One theory is that he killed the first victims to persuade Mary to change her lifestyle, but she found out and they argued, resulting in her death.

Francis Thompson, who failed at medical school and turned to writing poetry after an unhappy love affair with a prostitute.

James Kelly, who escaped from Broadmoor early in 1888 (confined there for the murder of his wife). He also spent time in America at a time when similar murders occurred there.

Dr William Thomas, a Welsh GP, was living in Spitalfields when the murders took place – but returned to his village (coincidentally?) after each murder. His suicide followed the last of the Ripper murders.

Lewis Carroll, the author of *Alice in Wonderland*, who is said to have revealed his guilt by coded messages in his book!

... AND THE RIPPER OFF THE RECORD

Commissioner of Police during the Ripper investigations, Sir Charles Warren, could have done better, to put it mildly. One of his bright ideas was to spend an extravagant £100 on a pair of bloodhounds, Barnaby and Burgho, who promptly became lost dogs and needed the police to find them.

The Ripper's crimes did not take place in dark, fog-filled alleys, but in the long clear nights of late summer and early autumn.

One victim (Catherine Eddowes) was killed on the same spot where a monk stabbed a woman praying at the altar of the Holy Trinity Monastery, before killing himself, in 1530.

It seems that one of the directors of the Bank of England dressed as a navvy during the night to scour the Whitechapel streets with a pick-axe, hoping to catch the killer.

Here's a clue: Jack the Ripper was left-handed. So that narrows the field then.

SOME MORE LEGENDARY EAST END VILLAINS

Jack Sheppard, the highwayman, was born in White Row, Spitalfields, in March 1702, and baptised at St Dunstan's. His short-lived career included an escape from St Giles Prison (through the wooden ceiling) and three escapes from Newgate, setting a record in escapology. He was finally executed at Tyburn in 1724, watched by 200,000 spectators.

George Smith, the 'Brides-in-the-Bath' murderer, was born in Roman Road, Bethnal Green, in January 1872. His three brides were all murdered the same way, all while on honeymoon, and all for insurance money, but George still had enough bravado to protest his innocence – before being hanged (in 1915).

The runner-up for the title of Prime Undiscovered East End Villain after the Ripper is probably Peter the Painter, the mysterious Russian anarchist who vanished from his Stepney address following the Battle of Stepney in January 1911. He and his Communist gang had been involved in the bungled jewellery burglary a month earlier (not their first crime), which resulted in the deaths of three policemen, leading to the 'Battle' (or 'Siege').

Jack 'Spot' (from the mole on his cheek) Comer, born in Myrdle Street, Whitechapel, in April 1912, made a fortune apparently from book-making, but in actuality from running a protection racket for East End Jews. He kept the Fascist blackshirts and others at bay under the façade of 'The Market Traders Association'. After having his face slashed in 1955 and again in 1956, he called it quits and opened a furniture shop instead.

The evidence suggests that Sweeney Todd, the demon barber of Fleet Street, was born in Brick Lane, Spitalfields, in October 1756. He spent some of his childhood in prison before becoming a prolific serial killer. Although charged with just one murder (of Francis Thornhill), 160 sets of clothing were found at his shop, and he was hanged on the 25 January 1802 and sent, ironically, for dissection.

THOUGHT YOU KNEW EVERYTHING ABOUT THE KRAYS?

Ronnie Kray never had fewer than 50 shirts at one time, rarely wearing one more than twice – and his socks were always of black silk.

When Barbara Windsor and the cast of *Sparrows Can't Sing* were filming around Cambridge Heath Road and other parts of the East End in the early 1960s, the Krays were hired to provide security on the set and can be seen – briefly – on screen.

The twins had a private masseuse and manicurist, and regularly visited a local gypsy to have their fortunes told.

When Reggie Kray married Frances Shea in April 1965 at St James the Great in Bethnal Green Road, the wedding photographer was Leytonstone-born David Bailey, who did the job 'for free'.

When Ronnie Kray shot and killed George Cornell in The Blind Beggar, Whitechapel Road, in 1966, the record playing on the juke box was 'The Sun Ain't Gonna Shine Anymore' by the Walker Brothers.

The Kray twins' trial at the Old Bailey in 1969 was the Old Bailey's longest criminal trial, lasting no less than thirty-nine days.

When Ronnie Kray's body was laid out at the funeral parlour in Bethnal Green Road in 1995, his dentures allegedly went missing. Well, he wasn't going to need them.

The final piece of music played at Reggie Kray's funeral at St Matthew's Church in Bethnal Green in 2000 was 'My Way'.

The Kray family burial plot is not in the East End, but is at Chingford Mount; and not only the Krays and their parents are interred but also Frances Kray, who – apparently – committed suicide in 1967.

Oldest brother Charles Kray died in prison in 2000 while serving time for masterminding a cocaine-smuggling operation.

LOCATION, LOCATION, LOCATION

Ratcliff Highway (now The Highway) was notorious as the site of four murders in December 1811, resulting in a reward of 500 guineas being offered. Three more murders took place half a mile away (in New Gravel Lane) just days later, acknowledged to be by the same perpetrator. While murder was not uncommon, especially in the area, these murders took place inside locked premises rather than on the public highway, and were regarded as a new threat to society. All in all, forty false arrests were made before John Williams (a lodger at the Pear Tree in Old Wapping) was placed in the frame, and his 'guilt' was accepted when he hanged himself in Coldbath Fields Prison, Clerkenwell. As a result of his suicide, his body was buried with a stake through the heart at the junction of Commercial Road and Cannon Street Road.

The Top O' The Morning pub in Cadogan Terrace, Bow, is just yards from the railway track where the body of murdered Thomas Briggs was found in July 1864, the first person killed on a train. He was taken into the pub, still alive, but died of his wounds, and his murderer Franz Muller was tracked across the Atlantic and caught as he disembarked in New York.

3 Nova Scotia Gardens (Spitalfields) was the home of two of London's body-snatchers in the nineteenth century, John Bishop and Thomas Williams. Their luck ran out when they took a suspiciously fresh, young corpse to the King's College School of Anatomy, alerting the police who found so much clothing on their premises that it suggested that literally hundreds of people may have been involved.

It was outside the Repton Boxing Club in Cheshire Street, Bethnal Green, that Freddie 'Brown Bread' Foreman abducted Ginger Marks in January 1965, later admitting to his murder.

The shoe shop don, Raffaele Caldarelli, was finally arrested in September 2006 (after ten years on the run) outside one of the shoe shops he owned at 5 Hackney Road (now Amore Tony Shoes). He had been living nearby for three years but had evaded capture in both London and Naples for charges of trafficking in drugs and arms, extortion and other Mafioso associations.

VISITING VILLAINS

When Charles II fell from favour in 1688, Judge Jeffreys, the notorious Hanging Judge, attempted to follow him overseas but was captured, disguised as a sailor, in the Town of Ramsgate pub (then the Red Cow) at Wapping. He was as frightened of the mob at home as he was of William of Orange's approaching army, and only the intervention of the militia saved him from much worse than being imprisoned in the Tower of London, where he died some months later, of kidney disease (April 1689).

In 1737, Dick Turpin stole a horse from Epping and hid him in the stables of the Red Lion at Whitechapel. When his partner-in-crime 'Captain' Tom King went to collect the horse, the law was waiting, and a gun battle followed in Goodman's Fields. As a result King was (apparently accidentally) shot and killed by Turpin, who then escaped.

A MEDLEY OF CRIMES AND CRIMINALS

Cowboy builders are nothing new, it seems. Thomas Slaymaker from Mile End Town appeared in court three times in the seventeenth century – for making poor joints, for defective bricks and for defective tiles.

Two Thames mudlarks (who made their living selling anything they dredged from the mud) from Rosemary Lane found that demand for 'antiquities' was exceeding supply so decided to make their own! William Smith and Charles Eaton produced the Billy and Charley forgeries (also known as the Shadwell Forgeries because they were said to have been retrieved from the Shadwell mud) in their own workshop. The fakes were mainly of lead and brass, shaped in moulds of Plaster of Paris, and bathed in acid to age them appropriately.

Medallions were the most popular seller, and they produced thousands of these, even though they were illiterate and many of the 'ancient' inscriptions were pure gobbledegook – but this was between 1857 and 1880, in the early days of archaeological advances. Nevertheless, they were caught and exposed in the end, but the law had no redress for their crime then, and they got away with it.

Young Patrick McQuinn made a minimal living in 1867 by cleaning the shoes and boots of gentlemen passing by his Leman Street pitch. But when Mr Abraham Woolf consistently refused to give the boy his custom, Patrick and his shoe-blacking chums resorted to violence. Having been struck down and kicked, Mr Woolf dragged the principal offender to the police station where he was sentenced to one month's imprisonment and hard labour.

Upon his return from Australia, Arthur Orton, the son of a Wapping butcher, tried unsuccessfully to convince the courts that he was the long-lost Baronet Sir Roger Tichborne (the longest trial, then, in British history: 260 days). This was in spite of Lady Tichborne's rather desperate acceptance of his claim; she was even said to have 'recognised' her son, who had completely different colouring and build and did not speak a word of what should have been his native French. He served ten years in prison, until November 1884.

When Messrs Spillberg, Nabian and Aaroris (*sic*) attempted to smuggle saccharin into their premises in Nelson Street, Stepney, they were trying to avoid Customs duty of about £500. The 2 hundredweight store of sugar substitute was concealed in wooden discs disguised as table tops, but was regarded (in 1906) as a 'drug' and the men were caught and charged with drug smuggling and intent to defraud Customs.

FAILED VILLAINS

William Brown broke into the New Baptist Tabernacle in Stepney Green in December 1868 with intent to 'commit a felony' but, in the dark, fell into a large cistern below floor level which had been used the previous evening to baptise several adults and not subsequently covered. When he finally managed to extricate himself, he found a bottle of port in the vestry to ease his troubles, and was found next morning in a state of 'complete intoxication' – and still a trifle damp.

Joseph Herrmann, a ship's cook, broke into 32 East India Dock Road while Edward Bartier and his daughter were sleeping. He helped himself to a number of dessert forks and spoons before finding a bottle of gin – and was found next morning, fast asleep on a couch, woken by the police constable who had been called out by the Bartiers. In his defence, he claimed the gin had been too strong.

Here Come The Girls

Joan Peterson of seventeenth-century Wapping started out by selling medication for headaches and curing sick cows (by counteracting malicious witchcraft). However, when one recipient didn't pay up, she turned to threats, causing – apparently – fits and prolonged illness. She was also, sadly for her, the owner of a black cat, and was even said to possess a 'familiar' – a squirrel. That was all the evidence needed to result in her being condemned to be hanged at Tyburn in 1652. Numerous books – and a play – have since been written about 'The Witch of Wapping'.

The seventeenth century being the century of witches, Anna Trapnel, daughter of a Poplar shipwright, was also accused of witchcraft – and madness. Her story was rather different, because she had had a spiritual revelation at the Church of John Simpson in Aldgate and became a fervent – and political – preacher. She must have made good use of her gift with words because she was released just four months after her imprisonment.

Damaris Page (*c.* 1610–69), described by Samuel Pepys as the 'great bawd of the seamen', moved from prostitution to running brothels. Apparently she had one brothel in The Highway for 'ordinary seamen' and one in Rosemary Lane for 'naval officers and gentry', although these were targeted in riots in the 1668 'bawdy house riots'. Her main centre of operations was the Three Tuns, and the Duke of York was said to be among her 'customers'. Although illiterate, she built several houses on Ratcliff Highway providing her with a life-long income, and she died a wealthy woman.

Elizabeth Gaunt, who lived with her husband in Whitechapel in the seventeenth century, moving to Wapping by 1683, was less lucky. A charitable woman, she arranged passage overseas for rebels, and carried messages for them over to the Netherlands. As a result, she was tried for treason in October 1685 at the Old Bailey, with one of those she had sheltered giving evidence against her. 'Mother Gaunt' was burnt at the stake at Tyburn just days later – the last woman in England to die so for treason.

Not content with her lot was Lady Ivy, born Theodosia Stepkins, famous for her wit and beauty and described as 'cunning in law'. After three husbands, she owned a vast acreage in and around Wapping and Shadwell, in addition to being settled with saddle horses and jewellery, but she wanted more, and took Thomas Neale (who leased the land from the Dean and Chapter of St Paul's in London) to court in 1684.

The judge was the infamous Lord Chief Justice Sir George Jeffreys. The lengthy and complex trial showed that Lady Ivy had forged a mortgage and counterfeited several deeds to substantiate her claim, and knew how to put saffron in the ink to make the signatures look older than they really were. As a result, Lady Ivy was tried for forgery, but was acquitted through lack of evidence against her personally, even though Judge Jeffreys commented on the witnesses who spoke on her behalf as being 'guilty of notorious perjury'. (The disputed land now makes up King Edward VII Memorial Park.)

Eliza Ross was a dealer in cat skins, who had no qualms about killing and skinning the cat of anyone who upset her (the landlady of the Samson and Lion in Shadwell for starters). Progressing from cat-killing, she murdered 84-year-old Caroline Walsh, a match-seller, in what is now Royal Mint Street so she could steal her clothes and sell them for a minuscule amount of money. Not surprisingly, this being 1832, she was hanged.

A Variety Of Punishments

When Ruth Herne broke into a house near Limehouse Bridge in June 1692, she got away with two silk hoods, two pairs of stockings, some lace caps and a pewter tankard, to which crimes she confessed. She was acquitted of burglary because the theft did not take place at night, but found guilty of felony and branded on her hand.

Thomas Gowen and Joseph Pewterer of St Paul's, Shadwell, offered no defence when found in Whitechapel Fields with some thirty yards of linen upon them, in August 1715. The linen – and a silk petticoat – had been stolen a few days earlier, and the two men were found guilty of burglary and felony and sentenced to death.

In 1783 John Hague was indicted for feloniously stealing a ham worth 6s and weighing 12lb from Strother Allen, a cheesemonger in Whitechapel. He was sentenced to be whipped before being discharged.

Ellen Morgan, aged 19, went into a hosiers in Shadwell High Street in 1834 and persuaded the occupant – Catherine Maher – to part, reluctantly, with 'several half crowns' to hear her astrological future. Ellen was arrested, following a complaint by Catherine, and, after a trial at the Old Bailey, was transported for 7 years.

Transportation for life was the fate of 20-year-old Samuel Rush who stole the following from William Reeves at St Dunstan, Stebonheath (Stepney), in 1841:

1 bottle-stand, value 25s
3 bottles, value 20s

1 cruet-stand, value 18s
6 cruets, value 12s
5 spoons, value 25s
1 coat, value £1 10s
1 blanket, value 1s
1 table-cover value 2s

23-year-old George Brown served 7 days' hard labour for treading on a constable's corn outside the Old Commodore Pub in Poplar High Street at the end of the nineteenth century. Ouch!

When Fred Manning and his wife were hanged in November 1849 for the murder of a Wapping moneylender, the execution was attended by thousands. Although hangings were a regular occurrence in Victorian England, on this occasion there was a certain Charles Dickens among the spectators.

In January 1888, James Cadderley attempted to steal a loaf from a baker in Bromley Street, but was caught and received twelve strokes with a birch rod.

LOCAL SCANDALS

Limehouse-born Mary East decided to abstain from male company when her boyfriend was transported to Australia for highway robbery. She felt more comfortable as 'James How(es)' and, as such, took over a pub in Epping with her 'wife' – but she lost her right hand following a brawl there. With the £500 compensation, the two women bought a pub in Limehouse, moving to the White Horse in Poplar High Street – but this proved less successful because here, her disguise as James came unstuck, and she was blackmailed. To the astonishment of many, she prosecuted the blackmailer, William Barwick, and attended court dressed as a woman, resulting in his being pilloried and imprisoned. However, Mary no longer felt comfortable and is believed to have retired to the country, where she died in 1780.

When schoolmaster Joseph Fisher of Bancroft's School, Mile End, complained to the school's trustees (the Draper's Company) about Elizabeth Fisher's infidelity with a colleague – John Entick, a widower – her defence was that her husband brought whores home to share their bed. The Draper's Company didn't need to hear any more and apparently solved the problem by dismissing Entick, and paying him the princely sum of £97 to leave the school immediately. No unfair dismissal cases in those days, however.

Brick Lane resident Joseph Merceron, a churchwarden in Bethnal Green (b. 1764), had responsibility for the Poor Fund but embezzled most of the money for his own and his family's use. He was also a magistrate with responsibility for licensing over a dozen local pubs (from the Ship in Brick Lane to the Bricklayers' Arms in Narrow Street, Limehouse), many of which were run as brothels, and did much to encourage bull-baiting and dog-fighting in the area. Even though he took care to employ only the ignorant to take care of any accounting, he was finally imprisoned in 1818 for stealing £951 1s 3d of public money. Surprisingly, perhaps, on his release some eighteen months later, he returned to his corrupt role!

When Granville Sharp lodged with his surgeon brother, William, in Wapping in the eighteenth century, he was working in Spitalfields (in the linen trade). However, after a chance meeting with one of William's patients, he became passionate about the abolition of the slave trade. The patient was Jonathan Strong, a teenage slave who had been so badly beaten and pistol-whipped by his Wapping owner, David Lisle, that his wounds were life-threatening and contributed to his early death at the age of 25. In the meantime, the Sharps paid for the boy's hospitalisation and found him paid work, but the boy was spotted two years later (1767) and seized again. Upon appeal to the Sharp brothers, a prolonged series of hearings ensued. The hard-fought campaign gathered momentum and its eventual success became key in the fight for the freedom of such slaves.

Charles Bradlaugh was born in 1833 in Bacchus Walk, Bethnal Green, and became an influential politician with radical views – he was an atheist, for instance, and he favoured birth control. In 1876, when living at Turner Street (Commercial Road), he was prosecuted for his part in the production of an 'obscene publication' (which was actually a book on birth control) and sentenced to six months plus a £200 fine. An appeal saw this conviction quashed, but his reputation suffered as a result.

When Horatio Bottomley (born at 16 St Peter's Street, Bethnal Green, in 1860) grew up to become a financier, and the Liberal MP for Hackney (1906), he began to abuse his power. He acquired some skill in fund conversion, swindling numerous people out of many thousands of pounds, and served five years' penal servitude from 1922 to 1927 as well as being expelled from the House of Commons.

In the early 1960s, artist Francis Bacon had a studio in Narrow Street, Limehouse. This was the studio that East End small-time crook George Dyer attempted to burgle – but was coerced into bed by Bacon instead. As a result of this meeting, the pair became long-term lovers, and Dyer was the subject of many of Bacon's portraits.

Not Forgetting The Good Guys . . .

The Marine Police Force, an early preventative river policing force, was founded in 1798 to deal with the theft and looting from ships anchored in the Pool of London and its surrounds. Armed with cutlasses and blunderbusses, it was the first organised (and salaried) police force in Britain and the first uniformed police force in the world, leading to the land-based Metropolitan Police Force. Its headquarters remain in Wapping High Street, albeit with a different name: the Marine Support Unit.

Jacob Tolhurst is remembered as one of the only river police officers to have been murdered – he accepted a poisoned drink while on his beat in March 1876 and died in St George's Workhouse less than an hour later.

Bow Road police station famously held Sylvia Pankhurst in 1913 after the suffragette was arrested for smashing windows. It is also famous for its original stables.

East Ender Julius Grant (1901–91), who studied chemistry at Queen Mary College, Mile End, became one of the foremost forensic scientists in the world. He was the man who verified that the Keating paintings, the Mussolini diaries and the Hitler diaries were fake. Earlier, he was also asked to analyse a piece of cloth from Tutankhamun's tomb, and he was called on to give evidence during the Great Train Robbery trial.

2

ROMANS, ROYALS & SOME RARE FINDS

III Unexpected Roman Finds

A signal station has been unearthed at Shadwell, which could have been used to warn of enemy ships approaching up the River Thames, and was in use until at least the fourth century. This was also where the remains of two leather 'bikinis' were found (!) preserved in a water tank, suggesting that the Romans swam here, before pollution set in.

An impressive dwelling was excavated in 2003 at the corner of The Highway and Wapping Lane, Shadwell, with ten rooms heated by a hypocaust system (the first under-floor heating) which was probably part of an extensive bathing complex. Oyster shells and the remains of geese, ox and beef carcasses also suggest that Roman soldiers lived the good life.

A substantial development has been uncovered in Old Ford (Bethnal Green), including wooden buildings, a barn, and cattle bones. The nearby river would have been the ideal place to transfer goods (from the north) to wagons travelling to London, and bones suggest butchery also for the London market. Indications are that a wooden bridge was built over the Lea before the river-bed was consolidated with sand and gravel for a firmer footing.

V Roman Roads

Ratcliff Highway (the Pretorian Way) is one of the oldest roads in London, originally a Roman riverside track between a lake fort (the lake later drained to form Wapping) and a red cliff (Ratcliff). A Roman bath-house was excavated here in 2004 at the junction with Wapping Lane.

Kingsland Road, just over the northern border of 'the East End', is what remains locally of Ermine Street, a Roman road from Londinium to Eboracum (York).

Old Ford Road once led to the ford of the River Lea and beyond – Lefevre Walk has revealed the remains of Roman houses in this locality.

Whitechapel Road once led to Colchester as did Roman Road, the route taken by Boudicca on her way to burn London.

(Note: these Roman roads were made mainly of gravel, which was quarried locally in Spitalfields).

VI Roman Cemeteries

Prescot Street, E1: the East London Roman Cemetery, with a significant number of burials accompanied by drinking vessels to ensure a squiffy send-off. Numerous funeral urns and silver have been found here over the centuries.

Spitalfields, E1: the remains of a high-status Roman lady dating back to the fourth century were found here in 1999, cocooned in a rare combination of stone sarcophagus and lead coffin. Small fragments of purple silk damask demonstrated conspicuous wealth as did jet and glass artefacts in the grave. At least a further 150 burials were revealed during the 1999 excavations, the preservation of the skeletons not always predictable: one grave contained nothing but feet inside a pair of hobnail boots!

West Tenter and North Tenter Streets, E1: possibly with the addition of a mausoleum. Roman artefacts and human remains dated to around the first century AD were found here.

Mansell Street and Alie Street, E1: an 1843 dig revealed human remains in a Roman burial ground where some skeletons had been burnt. Figurines of the goddess Venus were among the artefacts found here, as was a belt worn as a fourth-century badge of office. Coffins were of wood and lead. Excavation in the area in 1987 revealed a shallow Roman ditch which apparently served as the boundary of a cemetery or burial plot. A number of 'plaster' burials were found, together with a grave lined with tiles.

Hooper Street, E1: a 1988 dig unearthed bracelets and beads – East End bling!

'Radcliff Field' is mentioned in Stow's 1756 *Survey of London* as revealing the discovery of lead coffins a hundred years earlier, supposedly Roman. One with ivory and jet ornaments indicated a princess or a 'propraetor's' [magistrate's] wife.

POST-ROMAN FINDS

In 2000 a dig in Narrow Street, Limehouse, just yards from the River Thames, came up with china from Italy, Portugal, Turkey and Iran, seemingly buried – intentionally or otherwise – by Elizabethan and Jacobean plunderers. Forgetful, clumsy or just plain lost?

Developers on a site bounded by Artichoke Hill and Pennington Street (E1) found what is probably a seventeenth-century bellarmine [stoneware witch-bottle] complete with its charm. The charm seems to have been planned to counteract a witch's spell, and included the following ingredients:

A heart-shaped piece of cloth, pierced with three brass pins
Four fingernail parings
A quantity of human hair
Four hand-made pins
Several pieces of twisted wire
A handful of hand-made iron nails

ROYAL INTERVENTIONS

In 896, the Vikings made their way up the River Lea to build a fortress, but King Alfred – more than just a shocking cook – had the river blocked so that the longboats could not make their way out again.

Queen Matilda, wife of Henry I, took a wet tumble when trying to cross the old ford over the River Lea on her way to Barking Abbey, a favourite haunt. To avoid soaking the royal gown (or worse) on future occasions, she ordered a 'proper' bridge to be built, supported by three arched bows (*c.* 1110 – stood until 1835). The resultant bridge gave its name to the area – Bow – and the incident is commemorated in the nursery rhyme 'Skip to the Lee My Lady'.

Edward III, who got a lot more than wet when at sea and was afraid of drowning, pledged to build a monastery if he survived. The result was the Cistercian abbey of St Mary Grace built in about 1350 on the site of what later became the Royal Mint (between Rosemary Lane, now Royal Mint Street, and East Smithfield), a shift from prayers to pounds.

James I attempted to boost the silk trade in Spitalfields by planting mulberry trees (to feed the silk worms) but it seems he chose the black, instead of the correct white, variety. Whoops.

When James II originally gave permission for a May Fair to be held in the West End (near Piccadilly, hence Mayfair), he didn't envisage

that the Earl of Coventry would have the fair moved to Bow in 1746 (hence Fairfield Road in Bow.)

Charles II was more successful in 1682 when he granted Spitalfields a charter for a market to sell 'flesh, fowl and roots', a market which lasted until the twentieth century.

When Queen Alexandra was still a princess (in 1900) she presented the London Hospital, Whitechapel, with the first Finsen lamp seen in this country, brought from her native Copenhagen to treat lupus (tuberculosis of the skin). The ultra-violet treatment was used on 100 patients a day for twenty-five years, reducing its incidence. A statue and explanatory plaque remain in the hospital's courtyard.

ROYAL LEGENDS

Legend has it that King Edward III's hunting dogs (perhaps greyhounds?) were kennelled on the marshy Isle of Dogs in the fourteenth century. The legend remains as one of the explanations for the change of the area's name from Stepney Marsh to the Isle of Dogs, but is not verifiable.

Other English kings were said to have kept their dogs at the south end of what is now Cambridge Heath Road (known for a while as Dog Row for this reason) when residing at the Tower of London and hunting in Epping Forest.

Richard Brandon, who lived in what is now Royal Mint Street, is alleged to be the unwilling executioner of Charles I in January 1649, inheriting his job of hangman from his father. He was paid 30 crowns for the task. While it seems he was unable to forgive himself, he is also said to have removed an orange full of cloves and a handkerchief from the King's pockets, which he sold . . . Brandon went on to execute three further members of the nobility two months later, with the same axe, but died in June, reputed to be full of remorse.

Wellclose Square takes its name from a medicinal well which was allegedly popular with Charles II (the filled-in well now lies under the auditorium of Wilton's Music Hall).

There is some limited evidence supporting the claim that Quakeress Hannah Lightfoot from Execution Dock, Wapping, was the legitimate wife of George III. She was born in Wapping in 1730 and disappeared in 1753 – but the couple are said to have married in secret in April 1759 (before he was king) and to have produced three children. Records were concealed to allow him to marry Princess Charlotte of Mecklenburg-Strelitz in 1761. Hannah sat for the painter Joshua Reynolds, and, although the paintings remain, records of his sittings have also mysteriously disappeared.

The royal mistress of Edward IV, Jane Shore, does not seem to have died in an East London ditch in poverty, giving her name to Shoreditch! The legend lived on in the form of a Jane Shore Tavern at 103 Shoreditch High Street at one point, the same location where a painting of her was 'mysteriously' discovered.

Royal Residences?

In the fourteenth century, Edward the Black Prince (oldest son of King Edward III) used 'Poplar Manor House' as a residence on several occasions, no doubt a good place at the time for hunting and other rural recreations.

Bromley Hall on Brunswick Road, Bow, was seized in 1531 by Henry VIII as part of the Dissolution of the Monasteries. It seems he then refurbished this ancient dwelling, incorporating some spectacular tapestries, and used it as a hunting lodge. Tudor windows and a Tudor doorframe are still in evidence.

King James I (perhaps in common with King John four hundred years earlier) built himself a hunting lodge or palace in St Leonard's Street, Bromley-by-Bow, in 1606. The area was then a small, peaceful village and would have served as a retreat from the Scottish courtiers who had flocked into England following James's accession to the English throne. A ceiling and some of the panelled walls of this imposing, and sadly destroyed, 24-room residence have ended up in the V&A Museum in Kensington, complete with royal insignia – although this has not been accepted as definitive proof of its life as a royal dwelling.

As late as the eighteenth century there was a royal prince living in Petticoat Lane – Ukawsaw Gronniosaw, grandson of the African King of Zara. He changed his name to James Albert, not unsurprisingly, when he arrived in England after being freed from the life of a slave (he had been captured at the age of fifteen). James wrote the first slave narrative which was published in 1772, and married a widow who lived in the same lodgings – Betty – and who worked as a weaver.

UNUSUAL ROYAL VISITS

The Pretender to the throne of Portugal is said to have stayed in the Peter and Paul Tavern in Bow in 1591 on a visit to Queen Elizabeth.

In 1629, Charles I chased a stag from Wanstead to Nightingale Lane in Wapping, the sport watched by a scattering of locals who trampled over a local vegetable garden in the process. The stag was captured and killed but it is not known whether it ended up on the royal table.

The Aldgate tailor/merchandiser, E. Moses & Son, with its chandeliers and Corinthian columns, was well known enough for the deposed King of France to replenish his wardrobe there in 1848. Some sources indicate that it was this very Moses & Son that eventually became Moss Bros.

In 1856, King William Pepple of the Niger Delta (having been deposed following a power struggle in his home country) was baptised at Christ Church, Watney Street. At the lunch which followed, Pepple is said to have refused wine, preferring water. He was confirmed three years later and returned to Africa in 1861, financially compensated by the British government – at which time, in an attempt to bring Christianity to a people who still seemed to embrace cannibalism, he approached the Bishop of London with a request to send out missionaries.

The Queen of Holland visited Bethnal Green Museum (as it is now known) in 1872, reported in the *Penny Illustrated*, which refers to the absence of the usual 'half pint of porter or ale' being available for visitors, the museum only offering tea or coffee to 'offer no temptations to the ordinary working man and his missus.'

When Edward, the Prince of Wales, visited Limehouse in 1868 he wasn't interested in the docks; he was interested in the opium den run (legally, then) by Chi Ki – there's a pun there somewhere.

Helping Out The Royals

The nails for Henry VIII's *Henri Grace Dieu* were made at Poplar, and his *Mary Rose* was fitted out at Blackwall.

Henry VIII and his successors (Edward VI, Mary I and Elizabeth I) were all subjects for the royal painter, Levina Teerlinc, a Stepney resident. She was paid £40 p.a. and seems to have inherited her skill from her Belgian father, a fine illuminator. Very few of her valued (judging by her salary) miniatures have survived.

King Charles II appointed Thomas Neale of Shadwell his Groom Porter in 1684, and Neale held the post (in addition to being Master of the Mint) under the reign of William III. The job involved providing cards and dice for the gaming tables and deciding disputes at the card table or out on the bowling green. Neale had the power to suppress – or grant licences for – gaming clubs and to prosecute the unlicensed. As the spendthrift Neale died insolvent, it seems that gambling had something of a personal interest for him, as did property speculation.

(Sir Isaac Newton, his successor as Master of the Mint, found the establishment a 'nest of idlers and jobbers'.)

Roger Grant, although illiterate, was an oculist with a practice in Mouse Alley, Wapping. He had lost an eye in the service of the German Emperor in the continental wars, which he seemed to think qualified him for the job. He claimed to be able to cure cataracts 'in a minute' and forged the signature of minister William Taswell on a document claiming to have cured a blind man. Taswell had refused to sign because the man (Jones) had defective sight only and had not been cured. However, Queen Anne either turned a 'blind eye' as it were or fell for Grant's line of self-advertising, because she appointed him to her service – as did George I from 1715.

In the eighteenth century, Dr Richard Mead of Worcester House, Stepney Green, was appointed Physician-in-Ordinary to George II having attended Queen Anne on her deathbed a decade earlier. (Incidentally, the house where he died, in Bloomsbury, became the site for the Great Ormond Street Children's Hospital – his library was the first ward.) Mead came up with a recipe for Snail Water, a medicine for poor people who could not afford expensive treatments: its ingredients (apart from garden snails!) included juniper, aniseed, cloves, wormwood, spirit water and earthworms . . . all 'digested' for 24 hours . . . yum.

When Bow resident Dr Stratton Guinness (of the brewing dynasty) visited Nigeria in 1890, he met Prince (or 'Chief') John Mandombi who was suffering from a mystery illness. Dr Guinness, who had trained at the London Hospital, brought him there for investigations. He was admitted in October 1890, aged just 22, with an address at Bow Road (probably that of the good doctor) and admitted to George Ward where his illness was identified as sleeping sickness. Sadly, the prince died a few months later, but the research was very useful for future sufferers. A plaque – the Sleeping Sickness Bed Plaque – was erected in the appropriate location, but is no longer in evidence.

Queen Victoria's favourite yacht, *Fairy*, was built by Joseph Ditchburn of Poplar at his Blackwall shipbuilding yard.

George Doree, who lived in Alma Road, Bethnal Green (later Doric Road, presumably in his honour) in the nineteenth century, was one of the last Spitalfields weavers and hand-wove the 30 yards of crimson velvet used for Edward VII's coronation robe.

In 1928, King George V was treated with ultra-violet light at the London Hospital, Whitechapel. The carbon arc lamp that was used is preserved in the Royal London (Royal since 1990) Museum in Newark Street.

MORE ROYALS IN THE EAST END

A little unexpected is the 1545 tomb of nine-month old Henry Stuart in St Dunstan's – Mary Queen of Scots' baby brother-in-law who died before her husband, also Henry, Lord Darnley, was born. It is unexpected because it is a very long way from the Darnleys' Scottish roots. (Baby Henry was born at 'Stepney Palace' to the Duke and Duchess of Lennox).

After the Prince and Princess of Wales opened the new Institute for Seamen and Sailors at Poplar in 1894, they were known as the Pop'lar Prince and Princess. Did Queen Victoria get the joke?

QUIRKY ROYAL RULINGS

Patronage reserved for the Queens of England. This ruling applies to the Royal Foundation of St Katharine, started by Queen Matilda (1148) as a hospital east of the Tower and as a resting place for her two dead children. Queen Eleanor found it necessary to replace an embezzling prior in 1273, and the hospital/hospice was eventually moved out of the East End when St Katharine's Dock was built – but is back (since 1948) in a quiet part of Limehouse, still in use as a retreat.

When a Shoreditch man by the name of Barlow won an archery match at Windsor, Henry VIII awarded him the title Duke of Shoreditch, and subsequent London archers competed annually for the title.

3

LEISURE TIME

Penny Gaffs

Rough and ready (very) alternatives to early music halls or theatres, these were converted shops or stables opening onto the street with an improvised stage in a bare room. Whitechapel and Mile End Roads were particularly well endowed with penny gaffs. Many offered their 'shows' for less than a penny – a halfpenny, or even 'two ginger beer bottles'. One even offered free refreshments – although these turned out to be carrots! Luckily, East Enders have a sense of humour.

One particularly striking 'performer' was Mrs Douglas Fitzbruce who appeared variously as Godiva or Cupid in lively dramas, discharging mock fire-arms to add a bit of extra excitement. Other entertainments comprised such delights as human mutations – a man without arms or other skeletal deformities. Other politically correct acts included blacked-up minstrels. It was in one such place that the Elephant Man, Joseph Merrick, was discovered by Dr Frederick Treves from London Hospital in 1884 (259 Whitechapel Road). The penny gaffs died out at the end of the nineteenth century following new fire and safety rules and the growth of more spacious and comfortable venues.

A Dozen Lost Theatres – And One Survivor

Wilton's Music Hall, Grace's Alley, from 1858. It was constructed for 2,000 people but closed in 1880 as a result of problems with fire and safety regulations. Wilton's is reputed to be the site for the first can-can (which was promptly banned), and is the venue where George Leybourne (better known as Champagne Charlie) made his name. The Grade II listed building – including the original auditorium – survives as the oldest grand music hall in the world, although the original mahogany fittings have no doubt suffered, bearing in mind that it has since been used as a Methodist mission, a Second World War shelter and a rag warehouse. Thanks to a campaign by Sir John Betjeman in the 1960s, and to the Wilton Hall Music Trust (and 2009

talks with the National Trust) this could be the only music hall of 150 at the end of the nineteenth century to survive in the East End. Here are some of those less fortunate:

Goodman's Fields Theatre, near the junction of Leman Street and Alie Street, opened in about 1728 and staged several political plays by Henry Fielding. A new theatre with the same name opened in 1732 in Leman Street with a performance of *Henry IV, Part I*. David Garrick made his professional London debut here in October 1741, playing *Richard III*. Incidentally, a legend exists which claims that Garrick's later *King Lear* was based on a distraught father he met whose daughter had died following a fall from a window in Leman Street.

The Royalty Theatre, Well Street in Wellclose Square, opened in 1787 with *As You Like It*. It struggled with London's licensing laws, and tried another name from 1816 (East London Theatre) which seems to have been less popular in spite of the addition of gas lighting. In May 1825, it hosted the debut of African-American actor Ira Aldridge as *Othello*, a novelty for the British stage. (This was a performance he went on to repeat in Covent Garden eight years later.) The Royalty was replaced by the Brunswick in about 1828 after a fire (those gas lights) which destroyed hundreds of pounds worth of takings and put 200 people out of work. However, the new building collapsed during rehearsals just days after its opening, killing fifteen people and making it the shortest-lived theatre on record. It seems the builders had not taken into account the extreme weight of the iron roof! The failure of the Brunswick was hailed by some Puritans, among others, as a warning, and one clergyman apparently climbed onto the ruins to deliver a sermon against the wicked nature of theatres.

The Pavilion Theatre, Whitechapel Road, from 1828, was the largest in the East End until 1888, seating 3,500, and known as the Drury Lane of the East. Its stage was an impressive 70ft x 58ft, which must have been daunting for the six-year-old midget General Tom Thumb (Charles Stratton), who appeared in the 1840s. After being burned down in 1856 and bombed in the Second World War, it was finally demolished in 1962. Before that, it had served for a number of years as a Yiddish theatre, apparently being the venue for the first production of *Oliver Twist* – in spite of the stereotyping of Fagin's depiction.

Another theatre went up in Leman Street, the Garrick, at a time (1831) when it seems that there were nearly as many theatres as pubs in the vicinity. It was named after the actor who had made his London debut close by. Suffering a common fate, it was burned down in November 1846 and, although rebuilt, was finally closed around thirty-five years later and replaced – by a police station.

The National Standard Theatre, Shoreditch, started life as the Royal Standard which opened in 1835. It became one of the largest theatres in London, seating over 3,000 (the capacity declining in subsequent rebuilds, with variations on the name introduced each time). The great thespian Henry Irving appeared here, and opera was also featured, plus, a tad more low-brow, such acts as black singing conjoined twins (Milly and Christine, The Two-Headed Nightingale), on the bill in 1871. It appears that at some point after 1850, this theatre recreated Derby day and Ascot on stage using real horses – as many as fifty – who picked up speed in the adjacent marshalling yard before thundering across the stage! It became the New Olympia Picturedrome in the 1920s but was demolished before the start of the Second World War.

The Shoreditch Theatre (also taking other names during various revamps, e.g. the London Music Hall, the Griffin Music Hall, and the London Theatre of Varieties) was operational in Shoreditch High Street from 1856. Charlie Chaplin performed here pre-fame and fortune, to an audience of well over 2,000.

The Paragon Music Hall Theatre, Mile End Road, operated from 1885 to 1912, but also had a previous life as Lusby's Music Hall. One 1880 programme for Lusby's Summer and Winter Palace advertises both the Lupino Family, and a production of *Ulundi, The Zulu War*, featuring 200 highly trained children. It opened as the 'best ventilated' theatre in London, and the ventilation system, designed by theatre architect Frank Matcham, made him and his designs very popular. Charlie Chaplin (billed as the Hebrew Comic) and Little Tich were among its more famous performers. It was demolished in 1939 and rebuilt as a cinema, and remains as Genesis cinema (previously the ABC and the Empire).

The Royal Cambridge Music Hall, 136 Commercial Street, opened in 1864 with heating and electric lighting, seating 2,000. Destroyed by fire a few years later, it was rebuilt, complete with saloon, and – reassuringly? – over a dozen exits, but made way for a tobacco factory in 1936.

The Queen's (or Queen's Arms) Palace of Varieties in Poplar, from 1856, was revitalised when reconstructed in 1898 as a purpose-built theatre. Charlie Chaplin's name turns up again on the list of artistes appearing here, as does Gracie Fields. By the 1950s, this theatre was featuring a circus to boost ticket sales, but only lasted until 1964, when it was finally demolished.

The Wonderland, Fieldgate Street, Whitechapel, was reborn in 1897 for Yiddish productions, although there had been a theatre on the site for half a century under earlier guises: the New Garrick, the Effingham, the New East London Theatre, the Jewish Theatre. A particularly memorable show was the menagerie and circus of Christmas 1896, attracting some 45,000 people. At weekends, boxing came to replace the more traditional entertainments, which, incidentally, included some of the 'freak' sideshows popular at the time, e.g. the tattooed man, not so freaky today! This venue was rebuilt after a fire during the First World War but the revamp only succeeded in extending its life – as a boxing hall, a drill hall, and a cinema (Rivoli) – until its demolition in the Second World War.

Feinman's Yiddish People's Theatre opened in Commercial Road in 1912, in memory of the Jewish actor/playwright/singer Sigmund Feinman who had died in 1909. Although it housed 1,500 people, the productions were so lavish that the ticket sales failed to cover the costs, and it failed after just six months.

The Half Moon Theatre, Aldgate, from 1972 (in a former synagogue) moved to Stepney (a former Methodist chapel this time) and, after rebuilding, opened with *Sweeney Todd* in 1985. However, even with the endorsement of such local luminaries as Steven Berkoff, it closed for good in 1990. The premises now house a pub.

P.S. Brick Lane Music Hall is no longer in Brick Lane, it is near the Thames Barrier Park in North Woolwich, nearly, but not quite in the East End as covered by this book. It is the nearest example of real music hall, East End style.

THE EAST END'S BOXING HERITAGE

Legendary boxer Daniel Mendoza, born 1764/5 (accounts vary), started fighting in the streets to counter anti-Semitism and became known as the Father of Boxing with his revolutionary style of movement over strength. He was the first Jewish prize-fighter to become a champion (the 'Champion of England'), the lightest heavyweight boxer in history (160lb), the first boxer to receive royal patronage (following a significant 1787 fight which attracted the attention of the Prince of Wales) and allegedly the first Jew to meet King George III. Known as the Whitechapel Whirlwind, and the Star of Israel, he was more often billed as Mendoza The Jew. Even news of the French Revolution in 1789 did not knock coverage of his fights from the front pages of the newspapers. He retired in 1820, by which time he was already passing on his skills to the next generation, and ran the Admiral Nelson pub in Whitechapel Road. He lived in Paradise Row and then Horseshoe Alley, Petticoat Lane, where he died penniless in 1836. There are prints of him, as a bare-knuckle boxer, in scenes of the *Pink Panther* films, allegedly because Peter Sellers was a descendant.

'Dutch Sam' Elias was born in Whitechapel in 1775, and seemingly trained on gin. Known as the 'man with the iron hand' he lost only two of his 100 bouts, and is the inventor of the uppercut. His son, 'Young Dutch Sam', was English welterweight champion in 1825.

In December 1800, James Ward was born in Ratcliff Highway, the son of a butcher. He had his first fight at fifteen, but earned a living as a coal whipper (unloading coal in the docks) until his boxing became profitable. He became known as the 'Black Diamond', because of the inherent grime of his earlier profession, and reached his peak with a knock-out bout in July 1825, after which he received a belt proclaiming him as 'British Champion'. Upon his retirement in 1832 he became a publican, running a variety of hostelries including the King's Arms in Whitechapel Road and the George in Ratcliff Highway. Also renowned as a painter, musician, pigeon-shooter and quoits player, none of these skills proved profitable, and he ended up at the Licensed Victuallers' Asylum in South London.

Thomas King from Silver Street, Stepney, born in 1835, was coached by ex-champion of England Jem Ward at the George in Ratcliff Highway, and by 1863 had won over £4,000, enabling him to set up as a bookmaker. He went on to become a bit of a champion in a very different field – flower shows.

The first man to win a Lonsdale Belt was 'Bombardier' Billy Wells from Cable Street. Born in 1887, Billy went to Broad Street School in Shadwell, learning to box in the local clubs and East End missions. He took the British Empire Heavyweight title in 1911 after leaving the army to turn professional, and defended it fourteen times. Rather less famously, perhaps, he was the second muscular hunk to strike the gong at the start of Rank movies from 1948, also taking on a few 'bit' parts.

Ted 'Kid' Lewis (Gershon Mendeloff from Umberston Street, Whitechapel) began as a sparring boxer at just fifteen in 1909, at local boxing venues the Judean Social and Athletic Club (Princes Square), Wonderland (Mile End Road) and Premierland (Backchurch Lane). At eighteen, he became arguably Britain's youngest ever boxing champion (at featherweight) and the first to win a world title in the USA when he became World Welterweight Champion in 1915. Also known as the 'Aldgate Sphinx', he fought in six different weight divisions, resulting in thirteen other titles, with nearly 300 bouts under his belt, losing less than thirty (though records vary). Ted Lewis is also remembered as the man who drove an open car through the streets of Whitechapel throwing silver coins to the children, and is believed to have been the first boxer to wear a protective gumshield, designed for him by his dentist.

Teddy Baldock was born in Poplar in May 1907, and started boxing at Premierland, Backchurch Lane, encouraged by his grandfather (a bare-knuckle fighter) and father, a fairground boxer. At one point, he was billed as the 'Mumtaz Mahal of the Ring', the name derived from one of the Aga Khan's fastest horses. By 1927, he had enough supporters to fill fifty-two charabancs who watched him win the bantamweight championship at the Albert Hall. 'The Pride of Poplar' died in poverty in 1971.

Another Jewish boxer, Jack 'Kid' Berg (Judah Bergman, born in Cable Street in 1909) also began his career at Premierland, and went on to win the World Junior Welterweight title at twenty-one. The 'Whitechapel Windmill' became the British Lightweight Champion in 1934, and won three-quarters of his (*circa*) 192 fights. In retirement, he became a stunt man, living on (until 1991) to be the oldest British champion.

John H. Stracey, born in Bethnal Green in 1950, began boxing at the Repton Boys' Club in 1961. After winning five national championships, and competing in the 1968 Mexico Olympics, he became the World Welterweight Champion in 1975. Diversifying since retirement, he choreographed the fight sequences for *The Krays*, also coaching the Kemps for their parts as the twins.

Jimmy Flint was born in Wapping in 1952, turned professional at twenty-one and called it a day after thirty fights. Known as the 'Wapping Assassin', he taught himself to read and write so he could learn his lines to play the heavy in a number of films, and he produced a one-man play which was staged in 2008.

Although Charlie Magri was born in Tunisia in 1956, he was still a baby when he moved to Stepney, but much bigger when he won the World Flyweight boxing title in March 1983.

Newest East End hopeful Sam Webb (born April 1981), from the Isle of Dogs, took the British Light Middleweight title from Dagenham boy Anthony Small in March 2010.

Apart from boxers, the East End has other claims to fame in the boxing world – Repton Boxing Club in Cheshire Street (Bethnal Green) claims to be 'the finest boxing club in England' and York Hall remains the place for local boxing bouts. York Hall was voted the 'sixth best boxing venue in the world' by *Boxing News* in 2009 – alongside Madison Square Garden no less! Both local establishments started life as bath houses. York Hall still incorporates a bathing facility, now upgraded to a day spa, which won first prize in the 2007 Day Spa of the Year listings.

AND . . . Tania Follett made history as the first female corner at a York Hall promotion in December 1993.

FOOTBALL FOCUS

Isle of Dogs
In 1885, the Scottish jam manufacturers, Morton's, on the Isle of Dogs, formed Millwall Rovers FC, with mostly Scottish players. They used the Islanders pub as their changing room in the early days. Millwall was the only team allowed a 3.15 kick-off on Saturday, instead of 3.00, to allow supporters (often dockers, hence their early nickname 'the Dockers') time to get to the matches. They moved from Millwall to the Den in South London in 1910, but kept their Millwall name. (Note: the Millwall Brick is a weapon made from newspaper, so-named because of the team's later reputation for anti-social behaviour.)

Although Arsenal FC started life south of the Thames in 1886 (as Dial Square, a team of Woolwich Arsenal ammunition workers), they played their first match on the Isle of Dogs. That was against Eastern Wanderers, which they won 6–0, becoming Royal Arsenal soon after (December 1886).

Bethnal Green
Walter Tull became famous as the first black outfield professional footballer in Britain, playing principally for Tottenham Hotspur and for Northampton Town. However, he spent some of his formative childhood years (from 1898, when he was aged ten) in Bonner Road Orphanage in Bethnal Green. He was also the first British-born black officer in the army; sadly killed at the second battle of the Somme in 1918.

Bromley-by-Bow/Bow

George Hilsdon from Bromley-by-Bow was known as the 'Gatling Gun' because of the way he 'rattled in' goals. Born in August 1885 in Donald Street, he started his footballing life with Boleyn Castle FC and signed for West Ham in November 1904. In 1906, he scored five goals on his debut for Chelsea – a goalscoring record for a player's first appearance in the Football League. When he scored six goals in an FA Cup tie against Worksop, he set another record for the highest number of goals scored in an FA Cup match (later equalled by George Best). After returning to West Ham in 1912 he ended up as top scorer, but the mustard gas at Arras during the First World War ended his career, and he joined Fred Karno's vaudeville troupe in 1924, barely scraping a living until his death in 1941.

James Hird, born in Bow, formed the first football club in Russia for working class boys, the Odessa Football Club, in 1911.

Wapping

Danny Shea, born in Wapping in 1887, turned professional with West Ham in 1908 and was transferred to Blackburn Rovers for a record transfer fee of £2,000.

Limehouse
Sydney Puddefoot, born in Limehouse in 1894, came to prominence with West Ham and overtook Danny Shea's record when he was transferred to Falkirk for £5,000 in 1922.

Stepney
Ashley Cole, born in Whitechapel in December 1980, beat both of the above with a £5,000,000(!) transfer fee from Arsenal to Chelsea in 2006.

Some decades earlier, Sidney Bishop from Stepney played for West Ham in the first FA Cup final at Wembley in 1923 (they lost to Bolton Wanderers).

THE EAST END'S SPORTING PAST ...

Eighteenth Century
Bull-hanking. This involved cutting out a likely looking bullock from a drove of cattle and giving chase. A popular location was Whitechapel Road, but the introduction of a police force put paid to this particular sporting activity.

Bull-baiting, cockfighting and cock-throwing were all available. A 'Whitechapel bird' was then someone accomplished in dog-fighting, bull-baiting – and dog-stealing.

There was a bowling green in Wilmot Square, Bethnal Green, by 1787.

One particular horse race recorded in 1746 was between the Rose and Crown and the Spring Gardens. It took place over 20 miles back and forth along Whitechapel Road to Stratford, and the winner finished in 1 hour 11 minutes.

Nineteenth Century
The Mile End New Globe Cricket Club was formed in 1831, with the Victoria Park Cricket Club following in 1846.

A gymnastic club, the Orion, was founded in Mile End in 1868.

The Poplar Bowling Club dates from the mid-nineteenth century.

The Poplar and Blackwall Rowing Club was formed in 1860, with Bill Fisher victorious in the annual Doggett's Coat and Badge Race in 1911, other members following in his footsteps. It remains as the third oldest rowing club in Great Britain.

The Victoria Model Steamboat Club, the oldest of its kind in the world, started life in 1904, and still survives, holding over a dozen regattas at Victoria Park every year.

SPORTING RECORDS

Pedestrianism is, or rather was, a mixture of running and long-distance walking. A recent book by Paul Marshall (*King of the Peds*) features George Hazael [*sic*], the Whitechapel Walking Wonder, born in 1844, who became the first man to achieve 600 miles in six days, winning the equivalent of (today) £240,000 in prize money. There is also a reference to Bill Gentleman from Bethnal Green, born in 1833, who walked between 12 and 15 miles a day delivering cat meat (hence his nickname of Corkey the Cat Man) and earned cash prizes of around £10 apiece for winning races of between 1 and 10 miles in local venues, e.g. the Prince of Wales ground at Mile End.

Jimmy Lane, born in St Leonard's Road, Bromley-by-Bow, in 1884, was the British Middleweight Champion weightlifter and wrestler in 1902 and 1903. One bout, against the Russian Barney Shlitzer, lasted over 5 hours without a break or a fall – a world record. He became licensee of the Bombay Grab in the 1940s.

Brian Jacks, the judo champion from Stepney, broke the world record for squat thrusts in one minute (118) at the World Superstars Final in the Bahamas in 1980. A few months later, at the Superstars' Challenge of the Champions, he broke the world record for arm dips (100 in 1 minute).

Sarah Taylor, born in London Hospital, Whitechapel, in 1989, became the youngest female cricketer to score 1,000 runs in one-day internationals (in August 2008) and achieved the highest individual score against Australia by an Englishwoman in 2009.

On 23 May 2009, 1,675 runners broke the world record for the most people running 100 metres in a 12-hour relay. The event, for charity, took place at Mile End Stadium.

A very different world record – which could be classified as 'sport' – was broken in November 2009 by page 3 girl Rosie Jones at the Wapping offices of the *Sun* newspaper. She took her 30E bra on and off seven times in one minute!

AND SPORTING ANECDOTES

King Cole, an Australian Aborigine (real name Bripumyarrimin), was a member of the first Australian cricket team (all Aborigines) to tour England in 1868. He died of a combination of pneumonia and tuberculosis at Guy's Hospital in June, within a month of his arrival, the tour having apparently been marred by the team's home-sickness and drunkenness. Victoria Park Cemetery was, then, a significant and important burial site, and it is there he was buried (now Meath Gardens).

A horse named Bethnal Green won three races in 1872: Goodwood's Racing Stakes, Newmarket's Grand Duke Michael Stakes, and Newmarket's October Handicap.

Abe Saperstein left his native Whitechapel with his parents in 1907 when he was four. They arrived in the New World, and more than twenty years later Abe joined his local black basketball team (when teams were segregated), the Savoy Fives, who became, in time, the Harlem Globetrotters. Abe was elected to the Basketball Hall of Fame in 1970, four years after his death.

Another connection with the Harlem Globetrotters came in 1991 when the team thought they were saying goodbye to English basketball with their 'last' game: at the London Arena on the Isle of Dogs. Wembley, and other venues, have since welcomed them back, however.

The London (Docklands) Arena on the Isle of Dogs was demolished in 2006 after only seventeen years. Millions of pounds were spent, but, although it became home to renowned London basketball and ice-hockey teams with a capacity for over 12,000 spectators, the 1980s developers had not taken the lack of transport into consideration. (In contrast, the Docklands Sailing and Watersports Centre on the Isle of Dogs has had real success).

The London Marathon route, which includes 7 miles around the Isle of Dogs, was switched from a clockwise to an anti-clockwise direction in 2005. Three years later, the course through Wapping was diverted some 200 metres because of a suspected gas leak at the Old Rose pub on The Highway. The marathon runners also pound their way through parts of Limehouse, Canary Wharf, Poplar, and Commercial Road, before reaching the Tower of London.

Every Shrove Tuesday, Dray Walk is the centre for the Great Spitalfields Pancake Race. You need a team, and a frying pan, to enter – pancakes are provided for the heats and for the final, and dressing up is encouraged.

Exercising The Vocal Chords

With one of these cockney anthems:

'The Hokey-Cokey'
'Knees up Mother Brown'
'On Mother Kelly's Doorstep'
'Burlington Bertie from Bow'
'Any Old Iron'
'My Old Man's a Dustman'
'Run Rabbit Run'
'Boiled Beef and Carrots'
'Underneath The Arches'
'Two Lovely Black Eyes'
'Roll out the Barrel'
'The Lambeth Walk' (even though this is South London)
'Maybe it's because I'm a Londoner'

Or, with lesser-known 'tunes' of local interest including:

'Wapping Old Stairs' (a nautical ditty by Charles Dibdin, nineteenth century)

'The Shoreditch Toff' (nineteenth-century parody from Arthur Lloyd)

'Limehouse Blues' (1920s jazz standard)

'Chinese Laundry Blues' (a George Formby 1932 hit about Mr Wu from Limehouse)

And not forgetting . . .

'The Darlings of Wapping Wharf Launderette' (1967 Small Faces album)

'Mile End' (by Pulp in 1995, with a ref to Burdett Road)

'Cockney Girl' (unexpectedly performed in 2007 by American-born Chinese rapper Leehom Wang)

EATING – MORE PLEASURE THAN LEISURE

One hundred years after Samuel Pepys visited Bow to eat 'cherries and cream', a tea house is recorded in Blondin Street – the Clayhall Tea House. As a rural, fruit-producing area in Pepys' day (as was Bethnal Green 'village' where Pepys relished the good strawberries), this is potentially the same spot.

Joseph Malin opened the first fish and chip shop in England in 1860 in Cleveland Street, Mile End, expanding quickly into Old Ford Road, Globe Road, and further afield. However, it is reputed that Baroness Angela Burdett-Coutts, the East Enders' friend, was the one who had the original perception of combining the French idea of selling fried potatoes with the British idea of selling fried fish.

In September 1878, *The Era* published the 'bill of fare' available at Wilton's Music Hall, as follows:

Ham & Beef, 4*d* & 6*d* per plate
Pickled salmon: ditto
Oxtail in Jelly: 3*d* & 4*d* per plate
Carrots: 1*d*
Sandwich: 2*d*
Saveloys: 1½*d*
Fried fish: 1½*d* & 2*d*
Cheese & loaf: 2*d*

Pickles or sauce: 1*d*
Plum cake: 1*d*
Butter: 1*d*
Coffee: 2*d* per cup
Jewish Roast or Boiled Beef: 4*d* & 6*d*
Worsht: 2*d* & 3*d*
Collar bread: 1*d*

Tubby Isaacs' humble jellied eel stall on the corner of Goulston Street, Whitechapel, has survived since 1919. It is on the site of what was once a snuff house, which once offered a less fishy, but just as smelly, experience. Laurence Oliver and Vivian Leigh were said to be fans.

The first pie and mash shop in the East End, serving the same grub since 1915, is Kelly's in Bethnal Green Road. Confusingly, there is a second Kelly's in the same road which opened in the 1930s and is in direct competition.

Britain's most famous Kosher restaurant, Bloom's, opened in Brick Lane in 1920 and moved to Whitechapel High Road after the Second World War. It was famous for its food – and its rude waiters! Customers included the Marx brothers, Princess Margaret, Golda Meir, Charlie Chaplin – who stood in the queue like everyone else – and Frank Sinatra – who didn't. Sinatra had his meal delivered on a silver platter to the Savoy Hotel, but the silver was apparently never returned. Behind the scenes, it seems that Peter Rachman was a dishwasher at Bloom's before turning to rent racketeering! In 1996, Bloom's closed after a breach of Jewish dietary laws – it is now a Burger King.

The House They Left Behind was a pub (the Black Horse) in Narrow Street, Limehouse, so named because it was the sole survivor of the Blitz in this street. It is now described as a 'gastro eaterie' called, rather more briefly, The House.

During the 1999 Spitalfields excavations, the world's oldest bottle of wine was uncovered. Experts extracted tiny samples through the cork with a hypodermic syringe, and identified it as a very dry Madeira, from Portugal or Greece, dating from about 1679. It was found in the remains of the wine cellar of the Master Gunner of England, the house having been demolished and rebuilt in the 1680s, and its value was estimated at around £12,000.

In a Birmingham auction in 2000, a hot cross bun baked in Stepney in 1828 was sold to a Devon baker for £155 – making a claim as the oldest in existence; the bun, not the baker.

Fish Island (a conservation area between Bow and Old Ford) is so-called because of the local street names – Roach Road, Bream Street, etc. Appropriately, one local factory and restaurant sells rather upmarket gourmet fish: Forman's, who moved there when their original site was claimed by the Olympics upheaval (their customers include Fortnum & Mason). The Lock Keeper's cottage here was the site of Channel Four's *Big Breakfast* between 1992 and 2002.

Pellici's in Bethnal Green Road is one of only two twentieth-century cafés to earn a Grade II listing (2005). The Art Deco wooden panelling and floor are responsible, rather than the food. Choose pie and mash or pasta.

The Beigel Bake in Brick Lane is said to produce an impressive 7,000 bagels a night for its constant flow of customers (including Mariah Carey). Less well known are its cakes, such as elephant ears. Open 24 hours a day, it has competition a few doors away from the Beigel Shop, claiming to be 'the first and best'.

Gordon Ramsay has established a gastro-pub in Narrow Street, Limehouse, in a Grade II listed building which was originally a dockmaster's house. It is called, rather imaginatively, The Narrow. In 1997, Marco Pierre White also opened one of a chain of brasseries in Cabot Place East, Canary Wharf – no, not called Café Cabot, but Café Pelican. He also has a steak house in Petticoat Lane. Not to be outdone, one of the 'Jamie's Italian' chain from Essex boy Jamie Oliver opened in Churchill Place Mall on the Isle of Dogs in September 2009, the first in London.

Brick Lane has become iconic as the Curry Capital of the UK with around fifty Indian/Bengali restaurants, the curry close behind fish and chips as Britain's favourite food.

When Starbucks opened a shop in Whitechapel in 2007, a protesting crowd gathered outside to raise awareness about the chain's supposedly dodgy business practices resulting in the closure of local independent cafés. Police had to step in before the proposed East End knees up gathered any more momentum.

Parked outside the old Truman brewery in Brick Lane is the Rootmaster vegan 'bustaurant', inside a red London Routemaster bus.

Drinking As A Leisure Time Activity

The first bottled brown ale in England was produced at the Albion brewery (Mann, Crossman & Paulin) on Whitechapel Road in 1899.

Over 1,000,000 gallons of rum were lost in a fire at Poplar Rum Quay, West India Docks, in 1933, in spite of there being over fifty fire engines in attendance.

Legend has it that a sailor died in February 1720 after downing four pints of gin in one session at a Spitalfields pub. No doubt the same would happen if you tried it nowadays.

PUB STORIES

With a claim to be the oldest riverside pub in London, the Town of Ramsgate on Wapping High Street could date back to the 1440s. Originally known as the Red Cow, it changed its name because so many Kent fishermen unloaded their catches at Wapping Old Stairs. Apart from being the place where Judge Jeffreys is said to have been captured, its cellars were also a good place to hold prisoners awaiting transportation to America and Australia.

The Prospect of Whitby on Wapping Wall dates back to 1520. It was formerly known as the Devil's Tavern, but was renamed after the *Prospect*, a collier from Whitby which regularly moored nearby. Samuel Pepys and the riverscape painter William Turner are just two of the famous names known to have frequented it.

The Female Warrior in Wapping was named after Hannah Snell who ran the pub (no longer in evidence) for a few years after serving (*c.* 1745–50) in the Royal Marines disguised as a man. In spite of being whipped and wounded, she managed to maintain her disguise, having been searching for the husband who had deserted her when pregnant (unsuccessfully, as he was executed for murder). One side of the pub sign apparently depicted her as 'The Widow in Masquerade'.

Captain James Cook's father-in-law was the landlord of the Bell at Execution Dock, Wapping, in the eighteenth century, one of many frequented by press gangs on the lookout for drunks who could be easily kidnapped and sent to sea. Cook had met his wife Elizabeth Batts on a visit to the inn. But it was the Turk's Head nearby (now a café) which held the licence to sell pirates their last quart of ale on their way from Newgate Prison to the hangman's noose. The Captain

Kidd in Wapping High Street is a modern pub although named after the pirate who was hanged in Wapping in 1701.

In the seventeenth (and eighteenth) century, one of the ale-houses in Mile End Road was called the Why Not Beat Dragon. This reflects a Newmarket race when Why Not, a horse (obviously), beat Dragon – the winner reputedly owned by the Fenwick family, local landowners.

The Grave Maurice in Whitechapel Road dates back to 1723 (now the Q Bar at Grave Maurice), although it was resited close by in 1874. The name comes from Graf (Count) Moritz, a German Prince of Orange who helped the English beat the Spanish in 1600.

The Gun, a Grade II listed pub built in the eighteenth century, is not only famous for its Lord Nelson connection, but is said to house a 'secret' staircase complete with spy hole overlooking the river, used by smugglers looking out for revenue inspectors.

Landlords of eighteenth-century pub the White Horse in Poplar High Street were known as Mr and Mrs Howes until Mr Howes' secret was revealed: 'he' was actually Mary East. The only reminder of this early notoriety is the figure of the White Horse which remains, although the pub does not.

The Crown and Magpie in Aldgate was famous for its stone crown topped by a magpie carved out of pear wood – and trade (in the eighteenth century) declined when the magpie was removed, the pub being renamed Crown Beer. Trade picked up when the magpie was returned by its new owner, Benjamin Kenton. It was the previous owner of this pub who found a way of preserving ale on long journeys, building up a successful export business, which Kenton continued.

When Dr Barnardo bought the Edinburgh Castle pub in Limehouse in 1872, he had a different role in mind. He transformed it into the British Working Men's Coffee Palace. Whether he did a survey first is unrecorded.

The Still and Star in Little Somerset Street (Aldgate) is one of only two in the country with this name. Still probably derives from distillery, and the Star from the licensee symbol.

In the 1960s, Daniel Farson, the writer/journalist/presenter, set up a 'singing pub' on the Isle of Dogs – the Waterman's Arms (still in existence). Because of his celebrity status he was able to encourage top British and American names to not just drink here, but even to entertain – names such as Judy Garland, Shirley Bassey, George Melly, Tony Bennett and Groucho Marx. His great uncle, Bram Stoker no less, would have been proud – perhaps.

The Brick Lane pub the Frying Pan, once in the centre of the red light district, is now a Balti house, and the Lord Napier (same street) is now a Halal grocer. A sign of the times.

4

EARNING DOSH

Lost East End Industries

Aldgate slaughterhouses, Shadwell sugar making, Limehouse lime burning and Mile End's breweries were part of what were known as the stink industries of the sixteenth and seventeenth centuries, located just far enough from the noses of any West End toffs. There were glass factories in Ratcliff and Whitechapel in the seventeenth century, cigar and cigarette-makers in Shoreditch and Whitechapel in the nineteenth century, and brush-makers, rope-makers and basket-makers everywhere. In Bethnal Green were once businesses involved in such delights as manure processing (Charles Street – long gone), bladder drying (Three Colts Lane) and tripe boiling (Boundary Street). As late as 1938, there were over thirty butter and margarine factories in Stepney alone. Similarly, industries along the banks of the River Lea in the nineteenth century polluted the waterways: soap factories, paper factories and flour mills, confectionery factories and chemical works, piggeries and bone manure works.

In 1666, Joseph Truman developed the Black Eagle Brewery in Brick Lane, a company which went on to become the largest brewing company in the world in the nineteenth century. (It was also 1666 when the brewery supplied beer to the fire-fighters working in the Great Fire of London.) In 1737, when son Benjamin was in situ, the celebrations for the birth of George II's granddaughter were marred by the quality of the beer – so the Prince of Wales arranged a second celebration, with beer supplied by Ben Truman. It was the Trumans that came up with the first beer that could be brewed in large quantities without deterioration. This beer – porter – was selling 200,000 barrels a year. by 1835. Two other East End breweries from the eighteenth century have also bitten the dust – Mann, Crossman & Paulin's Albion in Whitechapel Road (1808–1959) and Charrington's Anchor brewery in Mile End Road (1757–1994), both of which were employers on a grand scale.

During the seventeenth century, the Bow China Works created a porcelain said to rival any, thanks to the local supply of cattle bones (from animals slaughtered for the City of London) which they mixed with clay. The company employed some 300 artists and workers until 1776 when everything was moved to Derby. Shorter lived was Limehouse Pottery at Limekiln Wharf, England's first soft paste porcelain factory, which survived from 1746 to 1748(ish).

By 1685, there were as many as 20,000 East Enders in the silk trade – before the famous Huguenots who settled in Spitalfields around this time following their religious persecution in France. The Huguenots set up their own hospital and churches which have not survived – but their presence lingers in street names e.g. Tenter Ground (where cloth was stretched on hooks, hence 'tenterhooks') and Fleur-de-Lis Street in Spitalfields, Weavers Fields (Bethnal Green), and Shuttle Street and Mulberry Street in Stepney, the mulberry being necessary to feed the silk-worm, even though the climate was not particularly conducive. By 1863, over 1,000 weavers had ended up in Bethnal Green workhouse alone, one of several workhouses in the area.

The largest rope works in Britain was Frost's of Shadwell (supplying the Thames vessels). Between Aldgate and Blackwall, there were four ropeworks in the 1740s, and rope fibres were once laid out ready for 'twisting' in Ropemakers' Fields (off Narrow Street, Limehouse). Ships' cables were also made in the area – hence Cable Street.

In 1865, an issue of *Penny Illustrated* refers to dripping-makers 'near Seabright Street, Bethnal Green' and in Backchurch Lane, Whitechapel, both 'flourishing' as evidenced by the owners being in possession of 'sleek cattle'. The chief ingredients were mutton suet and boiled rice with the addition of the gravy of 'bullocks' kidneys' when it is 'half cold' to give a mottled and natural appearance. Yum.

In 1901, fifteen Kosher butchers and poulterers were listed in Wentworth Street alone. By 1950, things had changed dramatically, and the first Halal butcher in Britain opened in Hessel Street, Stepney, another former location for Jewish food outlets.

Starting as a fertiliser factory in Millwall in 1871, the McDougall brothers soon made good use of the grain imports at Millwall

Dock. They turned to producing McDougall's Self Raising Flour, revolutionising home baking. The business survived into the 1980s. The Bow area was once known as the bakery of London, with the three mills at Bromley-by-Bow converted in the eighteenth century from flour milling to distilling, grinding cereal to produce spirits.

The furniture trade's London epicentre in the nineteenth century was in and around Bethnal Green. For instance, Ducal (famous for pine furniture) started life in Ducal Street. Of 135 businesses around Curtain Road in 1901, 102 were in the trade. Even the later London College of Furniture, Commercial Road, has now been swallowed up by the London Metropolitan University.

Quakers William Bryant and Francis May established their famous match factory in Fairfield Row, Bow, in 1861. They even produced their own labels for match-boxes, achieving numbers of some 40,000,000 per week. After they stopped using yellow phosphorus in production (one of the grievances prompting the Match Girls' Strike of 1888), they progressed to opening another factory on the site which survived until 1979 – it has since been converted into apartments.

William Booth (the Salvation Army man) opened a match factory in 1891 in nearby Lamprell Street, Bow, using safer red phosphorus, putting pressure on other match manufacturers. He produced 6,000,000 boxes of 'Lights in Darkest England' matches per annum but this was a short-lived exercise, closing in 1901 after he had made his point.

The Millwall plant for Morton's products in West Ferry Road, Millwall, from 1870, became famous for its confectionery and jams – in fact, the peppermints it produced were seemingly once used as a form of money in Madagascar! Morton's, taken over by Unilever in the twentieth century, employed hundreds in producing cans for all types of foodstuffs from vegetables to sausages and salt – even hair oil. The company was also the origin of Millwall FC, or, rather, Millwall Rovers, the name of the original 1885 works team.

Batger's also produced confectionery in the East End from 1748, employing as many as 700 people during the fruit season. Their output included sweets, jams, marmalades and cake decorations. They had two factories in Cable Street as recently as the 1960s – now artists' studios.

George Spill established a successful factory in Stepney Green manufacturing waterproof textiles, achieved by spreading rubber onto cloth. Nevertheless, he was more than surprised when given a government contract for 50,000 waterproof suits and thousands of waterproof fleeces for the army in the Crimea in 1855 – with forty days to produce the goods. The factory completed on time and opened other premises in East London, but didn't survive much longer after becoming embroiled in patent fights with the Americans.

The Natural Food Company in Cambridge Heath Road, Bethnal Green, became the largest wholemeal milling company in the country, producing 11,000,000 loaves per year. by 1911. It was taken over by a multi-national in 1971.

When the United Horseshoe and Nail Co. in Wharf Road, Isle of Dogs, won a Gold Medal in Antwerp in 1894 (in the 'Metallurgy of Iron and Steel' category), they must have thought they were well and truly heading for the big time. They were then producing 1,800 tons of horseshoes per year. But soon after came . . . the motor car.

The former Spratt's (animal food) factory at Limehouse Cut (active from the nineteenth to the mid-twentieth century) has been turned into up-market apartments. But memories remain of the fish heads being delivered by barge to make pet food, and of the millions of biscuits they produced every week during the Boer War for the British Army – presumably the non-pet food variety.

Edward Cook's soap factory in Meeson Road, Bow, had a range of prize-winning soaps by the beginning of the twentieth century (when the road had changed names). Throne toilet soap was described as having the fragrance of a 'Devonshire cottage garden on a lovely May morning' (!), their Eucalyptus soap was useful for 'sudden catarrh' and their Antiseptic soap had 'strong germicidal properties' – not forgetting their 'hygienic' Tooth Soap (!) which dissolved tartar and prevented decay.

The London Small Arms Factory was based in Old Ford Road, becoming particularly significant during the First World War when it produced components for famous rifles including the Lee Enfield. The location was close to the canal, on which parts could be transported from what was called Gunmakers Wharf to and from their other factory in Enfield. The Gunmakers Arms, now gone, reflected this industry, but the Gunmakers Arms Bridge remains.

East End street-sellers seen regularly until the twentieth century include cat-meat sellers (that's meat *for* cats), bagel sellers, the toffee man, the muffin man and the rag-and-bone man, the shoe black and the knife-grinder.

Success Stories

Anna Garthwaite, the daughter of a Lincolnshire clergyman, moved to Princes (now Princelet) Street in Spitalfields in 1729 after her father's death. This was a time when the area was renowned for its silk production. With an interest in textiles, she was able to work with master weavers, becoming widely renowned for her work with flowered silk designs, some of which survives in the collections of the Victoria & Albert Museum in London.

Quaker William Allen, born in Steward Street, Spitalfields in 1770, was to become famous as a part of Allen & Hanburys, the pharmaceutical giants. He invested a good part of his time – and cash – in supporting the abolition of slavery and of capital punishment. A century later, the company he started had large premises in Three Colts Lane, Bethnal Green, and expansion continued – in spite of the building being destroyed in the First World War – until they were taken over by Glaxo in 1958, the name being discontinued in 1978. The company came up with a number of innovative ideas during its lifetime, including the double-ended baby feeder.

Charles Henry Harrod from Rosemary Lane founded a tea emporium and wholesale grocers at 4 Cable Street in 1835. Less than thirty years later, he expanded into Knightsbridge – and everyone knows what happened next.

John Knight won a medal at the Great Exhibition of 1851 – having produced soap in his Wapping factory since 1836. His name lives on in Knight's Castile soap.

Precocious William Perkin entered the Royal College of Chemistry at just fifteen, and had invented the first alkaline dye (mauveine – or you could say he discovered the colour purple) by the age of eighteen. He was born in King David's Lane, Shadwell, in 1838, and did his initial research at Gosling House, Cable Street, before moving on to bigger and better things. His knighthood, shortly before his death, was the last in a chain of awards after he had introduced other new colours (violet – favoured by Queen Victoria – and specific shades of red and green), and he died a very rich man.

When Jack Cohen (born in Rutland Street in 1898) started selling such goodies as fish paste and golden syrup from a Brick Lane market stall after the First World War, did he think he'd end up establishing Tesco?

Blackman's, the tiny shoe shop in Cheshire Street, Bethnal Green, was started in the 1930s, and is the longest-running business in the street. It was famous in the 1960s as the first British suppliers of Doc Marten shoes (mainly to skinheads at the time) and is still famous now – for its plimsolls.

The Billingsgate Fish Market is the UK's largest inland fish market and its largest shellfish market. Some 25,000 tons of fish and fish products are sold each year from around 50 merchants, assisted by 150 porters. It was moved from its ancient City of London home to 13 acres on Trafalgar Way on the Isle of Dogs in 1982, partly due to complaints from the pin-striped City types.

UNEXPECTED INSIGHTS

England's first mahogany staircase was carved by Marmaduke Smith, a Spitalfields carpenter. It was installed at the house he built for himself at no. 4 Church Street (now Fournier), Spitalfields, in 1726.

The silk for Queen Victoria's coronation gown was woven at no. 14 Church Street, Spitalfields.

East Enders who wanted to learn traditional skills such as jewellery or cabinet-making were catered for when the Guild of Handicraft set up its operation in Toynbee Hall, Whitechapel, in 1888, with up to 1,000 people attending classes, concerts and lectures on a weekly basis. (The YHA in 1929 and the WEA in 1903 were both launched from Toynbee Hall.) The People's Palace in Mile End Road also offered instruction in woodcarving, electrics, dressmaking, tailoring and clay modelling.

The suffragette Sylvia Pankhurst founded a nursery and a toy factory (to give employment to local women) in Norman (now Grove) Road, Bow, not far from her HQ. She also refurbished the Gunmaker's Arms on the corner of Old Ford and St Stephen's Roads and renamed it the Mothers' Arms – not a pub but a mother-and-baby clinic.

In the 1930s, Spiegelhalter's jewellers in Whitechapel Road refused to make way for the construction of Wickham's Department Store (the 'arrods of Whitechapel), so they built round it, leaving the jewellers in solitary splendour in the middle.

The Grade II listed Poplar Town Hall (now a business centre) on the corner of Fairfield and Bow Roads features five exterior carvings that represent the labourers who built it – architect, stonemason, navvy, carpenter and welder.

Advertising Their Wares In *The Penny Illustrated* (Nineteenth Century)

St Jacob's Oil, produced by Henley's, Commercial Road, was described as 'curing' such ailments as gout, rheumatism, sciatica, and neuralgia virtually overnight. The company published letters from happy customers, the majority from postmen who 'whether suffering or not . . . are obliged to be at their post'. Nice bit of marketing.

Cope's Tobacco Company (Columbia Market) claimed to do 'more for the welfare of Bethnal Green than any Lady Bountiful' by employing a 'host of girls . . . rolling cigars [from] fragrant tobacco leaves . . .' and by offering 'good wages and pleasant employment'. The Smoking Kills message had not yet sunk in.

Madame Victor's Imperial Face Bloom 'takes ten years off one's age . . . It makes one more welcome in every society, while the youth of both sexes may make more successful matrimonial alliances by its use and aid'! A bargain, surely, at only 4s 9d in stamps to their Approach Road address in Bethnal Green.

Even cheaper were the free samples of 'Flowers of Rice Soap' made from vegetable oils and rice powder, warranted 'to impart whiteness and beautiful surface to the skin'. These were available from Albany Soap Works, Grosvenor Street, Stepney.

'Scurf of the head' could be relieved by sending just 9d to Rogers the Chemist in Ben Jonson Road, Stepney. In return, they would send a packet of Roger's Furfurine, guaranteed to 'remove every particle and allay the irritation'.

Surviving Industry

The Whitechapel Bell Foundry is Britain's oldest manufacturing company (dating from 1570) and is still going strong in Whitechapel Road. The most famous bells it has produced include the clock bells of St Paul's Cathedral (1709), the original Liberty Bell (1752) and the 13-ton Big Ben (1858), the largest ever cast at the foundry. The latter bell needed sixteen horses to haul it to Parliament Square. It is one of only two such businesses in the country and the historic premises are Grade II listed. A lesser known bell, but just as fascinating, was the Operation Bell provided for the London Hospital in 1791 – it is reputed to have summoned attendants to hold surgical patients still before anaesthetics were introduced in 1846.

On a smaller scale, the last furrier in Spitalfields remains at Gale Furs, a business dating back to 1963 when the fur trade was at its height. Creative locals Gilbert and George have their fur collars and hats made here.

Newer Arrivals In The East End

The Canary Wharf initiative

93,000 people – and rising – work in Canary Wharf, the twenty-first century face of the East End. Canary Wharf is a founder member of the UK Green Building Council, championing sustainable building design. The first tenants, US finance company State Street, moved into the Wharf in August 1991. Apart from the impact of the service industries which have moved to the area, there is 740,000sq ft of retail space, making it one of the largest shopping centres within the M25. The first retailer, in 1999, was Boots, but rapid expansion has resulted in 90 shops, 65 food outlets and 3 supermarkets in Canary Wharf.

Banks in Canary Wharf:

ANZ Bank
Bank of America
Bank of NY Mellon Corporation
Barclays Bank
China Construction Bank
Clydesdale Bank
Coutts & Co.
Credit Suisse
HSBC
Morgan Stanley
JP Morgan (en route)
NatWest

Nomura International
Saxo Bank
Wells Fargo

NEWS IS GOOD NEWS

The *Telegraph* group moved from Fleet Street, EC4, to South Quays, Isle of Dogs in 1987 and then to Canary Wharf tower in 1991. *The Times, Sunday Times, News of the World* and the *Sun* changed location from offices in Holborn and Fleet Street to one site in Wapping in 1986. The *Mirror* moved its base from Holborn Circus to the Canary Wharf tower in 1994. The *Independent* switched from City Road EC1 to the Canary Wharf tower in 1994, moving to Marsh Wall in Docklands in 2000 (although they have since moved – again! – out of the area to the HQ of Associated Newspapers in a cost-cutting exercise).

THE PHENOMENON THAT IS NO. 1 CANADA SQUARE

The 36ft lobby incorporates 90,000sq ft of Italian and Guatemalan marble.

The tower has 4,388 steps and, luckily, 32 passenger lifts which travel the 50 floors in 40 seconds.

There are 3,906 windows in the tower which used 27,500 tons of British steel in its construction.

The building is able to sway 13.75 inches to allow for strong winds.

The aircraft warning light at the top of the tower flashes forty times a minute (the nearest airport is London City Airport, East Ham).

MORE NEW ENTERPRISES

The Old Truman Brewery in Brick Lane now houses a range of creative businesses (not to mention bars and exhibitions) including

Fashion East which was started in 2000 to showcase local designers. Among other similar artistic local enterprises, Rich Mix in Bethnal Green Road has produced women's wear label Erdem, one of whose creations was worn by Sarah Brown (Mrs Gordon Brown of course) at London Fashion Week in 2010.

In the 1980s, City Cruises started out as a family business run by two generations of the Beckwiths from the Isle of Dogs. It has become such a success that it was named regional winner in the Best UK Family Business Awards in 1996 and lays claim to being the largest riverboat operator on the Thames, with fourteen cruisers. The first new sight-seeing vessel on the Thames for twenty-five years, the *Millennium of London*, was christened by the Queen in October 1996, with several added since. Over a million passengers a year enjoy the fruits of the Beckwiths' labours.

The Aitch Group are building a 252-bedroom hotel in West India Dock Road, to be completed in time for the 2012 Olympics, much of which is taking place just a whisker away.

ETHNIC FIRSTS

The first Asian grocery store in the UK, the Taj Stores, was established in Brick Lane in 1930.

The first Asian to get a job in a Wimpy bar was Shafiq Uddin, then living in Heneage Street, Stepney. He was taken on by the Jewish manager of the Whitechapel outlet at the end of the 1950s.

London's first weekly Bengali newspaper, *Janomot*, was established in 1969 at Chicksand Street, Whitechapel.

The new millennium was marked by the opening of the first Bangladeshi bank in the UK – the Sonali Bank in Osborn Street, Aldgate.

The Bangladesh Olympic 2012 team is setting up a training base in Tower Hamlets, in the heart of the Bengal community.

5

PEOPLE

NAMES TO CONJURE WITH

(Suggest some allowances be made for dodgy handwriting in parish registers …)

Birth records
Fanny Funk, Whitechapel, 1859
George James Cockhead Cockhead, St George in the East, 1860
    (a double whammy)
Rose Bush, Shoreditch, 1864
Eleazer Bed, Whitechapel, 1871
Tommy Rot, Shoreditch, 1871
President Percy Smith, Poplar, 1881
Lilian Fluffy Barrett, Shoreditch, 1895
Scott Free, Bethnal Green, 1901
Zipporah Moonshine, Mile End Old Town, 1908
Wolf Bear Chalvony, St George in the East, 1910
Roger Caesar Marius Bernard de Delgado Torres Castillo Roberto,
    Whitechapel, 1918*

Baptism records
Oliver Slowcock, Whitechapel, 1778
Thomas Turd, Bethnal Green, 1788
Ben Dover (think about it), St George in the East, 1839

Marriage records
Sapiens Upright, St Dunstan's, 1667
Dick Slippery, St Dunstan's, 1675
Geronimo Bow, St George in the East, 1810
Anna Rack, St George in the East, 1881
Choo Ah Beano, Stepney, 1882

---

* used the name Roger Delgado in his acting career, featuring in such roles as The
Master in *Dr Who*.

Death records
Captain Manship, Mile End (aged 96), 1786
Eliza Scavenger, Stepney, 1839
Otter Otters, Mile End, 1868
Poo Out, Stepney, 1888

Census records
Bagel Baker, Shoreditch, 1841 (*surely* the wrong column?)
Cold Pacific, Bow, 1881
Dick Less, Limehouse, 1891
Dude Sugarberg, Mile End, 1901
Justa Crook, Mile End, 1901

PEOPLE MAKING MUSIC IN THE EAST END

In 1886, Lady Colin Campbell was attributed with a crowd of 20,000 fans milling around when she sang at the Cottage Mission Hall in Limehouse. As this was shortly after her scandalous divorce – the first in Britain thanks to new legislation – with its revelations of her sex life and her husband's syphilis, the question is: did the mob come to listen to her sing, or . . .

Dan Leno, the biggest name in Victorian music hall, made his London debut in 1885 at the Foresters' Music Hall in Cambridge Heath Road, (a cinema from 1925 to 1960) as the champion clog dancer of the world. However, it seems the audience were not impressed and he had to win them over by singing.

Although Charles Coborn, the music hall star responsible for such gems as 'The Man Who Broke the Bank at Monte Carlo', was born in Mile End, he took his stage name from Coborn Road, Bow (birth name Colin McCallum).

Someone who managed the move from music hall to recording artiste was Issy Bonn, born Benjamin Levin in Brick Lane in 1893. He made his stage debut at the Mile End Empire and has two rather different main claims to fame: the hit 'My Yiddisher Momma', and appearing on the cover of the Beatles' *Sergeant Pepper* album.

Dick James was born Richard Leon Isaac Vapnick in Underwood Street, Spitalfields, in 1920. If the name does not mean a lot, then the Beatles and Elton John may ring bells. James was the man who set up a music publishing company at just the right time – 1961 – and published songs by both acts at the beginning of their careers, becoming a multi-millionaire as a result. Before that, his main claim to fame was recording the theme tune to *The Adventures of Robin Hood* which notched up nearly 150 episodes. All together now: 'Robin Hood, Robin Hood, riding through the glen, Robin Hood, Robin Hood, with his band of men. . . .'

Billy Ocean worked for a Brick Lane tailor before finding musical success. Not far away, in the 1960s, Paul Simon (of Simon and Garfunkel) lived in Cable Street with his English girlfriend, Kathy ('Kathy's Song').

Ballad singer, Tex, the East End Cowboy, was a favourite at the Rising Sun in Bethnal Green in the 1970s with his massive Stetson, and in spite of his hunchback. He was on occasion accompanied on stage by his white horse!

In 1981, the winner of the Eurovision Song Contest was 'Making Your Mind Up' with Bucks Fizz, featuring Cheryl Baker. More recently a television presenter, Cheryl was born Rita Crudgington in Bethnal Green and brought up in a council flat.

Pete Doherty lived in Teesdale Street, Bethnal Green, in the formative years of The Libertines, whose video of 'Up The Bracket' was filmed in nearby Hare Row. He rechristened the run-down Victorian terrace the Albion Rooms in spite of its reputation as 'a tip'.

2006 saw Madonna celebrating her 48th birthday at Lounge Lover, a glitzy bar in a gritty area – Whitby Street, off Brick Lane.

Devonshire Square off Petticoat Lane was the site, in June 2009, for 850 ukulele players strumming their way into *The Guinness Book of Records*, watched by thousands. They doubled the previous record.

Both Dizzee Rascal and Tinchy Stryder, twenty-first-century grime stars, hail from Bow. However, Chas 'n' Dave, originators of 'rockney' music are not East Enders: they are actually from North London.

TEN MORE WELL-KNOWN MUSICAL NAMES

Marie Lloyd, music hall star, was born in Plumber Street, Shoreditch, in 1870 as Matilda Wood. On her death in 1922, pubs in the East End were draped in black crêpe in her honour.

Bud Flanagan OBE, was born Chaim Reuben Weintrop in Hanbury Street, Spitalfields, in 1896. As a twelve-year-old, he is reputed to have *walked* to Southampton to join a ship that would take him to America, where he joined a vaudeville act. Returning to the UK after serving in the First World War, he met up again with Chesney Allen (a war comrade) and became a huge success as part of Flanagan and Allen and part of the Crazy Gang on stage and film. His voice is still heard in *Dad's Army*'s theme tune 'Who Do You Think You Are Kidding, Mr Hitler?'

Band leader Joe Loss – signature tune 'In the Mood' – was born in Grey Eagle Street, Spitalfields, in 1909 and educated at the local Jewish Free School. He became Britain's youngest band leader, EMI's longest-serving artist and played at the wedding balls for Princesses Margaret, Alexandra and Anne.

Ronnie Scott, as famous for his club as for his musical talent, started life in the maternity hospital in Commercial Road, Stepney (long gone), in January 1927.

Lionel Bart (1930–99), the songwriter and composer responsible for *Fings Ain't Wot They Used T'Be*, *Oliver!*, etc., hails from Underwood Road, Whitechapel, where he started life as Lionel Begleiter. The name Bart is said to have been chosen after he often passed Bart's Hospital on the bus travelling from Whitechapel to St Martin's School of Art. He claims to have written 'Living Doll' in just six minutes, the first million-selling single in Britain. As a result of his musical know-how he was a millionaire by 1960, but his business know-less meant he was bankrupt in the 1970s.

Matt Monro, the singing bus driver who had, among others, the 1963 hit 'From Russia With Love' (also written by Lionel Bart) was born in Shoreditch on 1 December 1930.

Des O'Connor was born in Stepney in 1932 – that's if 'Dick-a-dum-dum' counts as 'music'.

Alma Cogan was born in Whitechapel – according to her sister, anyway – in 1932, although the family moved out of the area before she was eight years old. She had more hits (eighteen) than any other female singer in the 1950s.

Helen Shapiro, 1960s singing sensation ('Walking Back to Happiness' etc.) was born in Bethnal Green Hospital because there was no room at her local hospital in Hackney when she arrived on 28 September 1946, six weeks early.

Kenny Jones, drummer with The Small Faces and The Who, was born in Stepney in September 1948 and lived near Shadwell Park. He now owns a polo club in Surrey.

FIVE WRITERS BORN IN THE EAST END

Edmund Spenser was born in about 1552 between East Smithfield and Rosemary Lane. Among the many works he left behind for posterity, the most famous is probably *The Faerie Queen*, his allegorical masterpiece.

Arthur Morrison was born in John Street, Poplar. He wrote *Tales of the Mean Streets* (1894) as a collection of short stories, featuring the East End, but, after visiting the Old Nichol slum area in Bethnal Green, he wrote *Child of the Jago*, exposing the localised poverty and conditions. His biggest success was *Hole in the Wall* (1902), set in Wapping.

Peter Cheyney, author of thirty-four crime novels, was born in 1896 at 92 Whitechapel High Street, the ground floor of which was his mother's corset shop. His books sold millions in the 1930s and '40s, and many were made into films.

Wolf Mankowitz (1924–98) was born in Fashion Street, Spitalfields. His success with such musicals as *Expresso Bongo*, novels such as *A Kid for Two Farthings*, and film scripts such as *Casino Royale* followed his initial career in antiques, when he was joint editor of the *Concise Encyclopedia of English Pottery and Porcelain.*

Bernard Kops, born in Stepney in 1926, is one of Europe's best known Jewish playwrights, starting with *The Hamlet of Stepney Green* in 1958. Brought up in Stepney Green Buildings, Bernard has added not only to his impressive repertoire as a playwright (forty plays to date) but has nine novels and seven volumes of poetry under his belt – many with his East End background as the subject matter, e.g. *Whitechapel Library, Aldgate East.*

FIVE ARTISTS BORN IN THE EAST END

William James Blacklock was born in Shoreditch in March 1816. The family moved to Cumberland when he was just two, and this is where he established himself as a celebrated landscape painter, becoming known as the 'painter of Cumberland'.

Mabel Lucie Attwell was born in Mile End Road in 1879, and became the breadwinner for her family after her husband was wounded in the First World War. Her success was the result of her wealth of illustrations for such famous works *as The Water Babies, Alice in Wonderland* and *Grimm's Fairy Tales.*

Mark Gertler, born in extreme poverty to a Jewish family in Spitalfields in 1891 but with a precocious talent, won a scholarship to the Slade School, and went on to produce fine portraits, with other work including the modernist anti-war painting 'Merry Go Round'. It is said that Gertler was the model for the sculptor in *Women in Love* by D.H. Lawrence. After an unhappy love affair, prolonged illness, constant clashes between his own conflicting views in religion and in class, and a dissatisfaction with marriage and fatherhood, he committed suicide in 1939.

William Larkins, born in Bow in 1901, won a scholarship to Goldsmith's College and went on to specialise in etchings of the East End, which did well in the 1920s until etchings went out of fashion. Switching, wisely, to the world of advertising, he was the man behind the Black Magic chocolate box, the Aero wrapper and the Lux soap flakes box.

Also born in 1901 (in Stepney) was Barnett Freedman, who won a scholarship to the Royal College of Art. It was Freedman who designed the stamp to celebrate the Silver Jubilee of King George V in 1935, and his name can be seen on many London transport posters. Additionally, he was an official war artist during the Second World War, and some of his paintings still hang in London's Tate and V&A.

A DOZEN ACTORS BORN IN THE EAST END

Victor McLaglen (1886–1959) was born in Commercial Road but escaped from his large family by joining the Life Guards before his fifteenth birthday, necessitating a white lie. He became the boxing champion of the regiment, resulting in exhibition work in the USA in circuses and Wild West shows. After joining the Gold Rush in Australia, he returned to boxing at home but was offered his first film role in 1920 (*The Call of the Road*). A further sixty films followed, with co-stars including Mae West, Marlene Dietrich and Barbara Stanwyck. One of those actors with an unfamiliar name – even though he won an Oscar for Best Actor in 1935 for *The Informer* – but a familiar face.

Jack Warner OBE (1895–1981) was born Horace Waters in Poplar and educated at Cooper's Company School in Mile End Road. After the First World War he became a cabaret singer and professional comedian, following in the footsteps of his sisters (Elsie and Doris Waters, the variety comediennes known as Gert and Daisy), but not trading on their name. Jack progressed from music hall through radio and film to his iconic role as *Dixon of Dock Green*, which he assumed from 1955 to 1976, a total of 432 episodes starting in black and white and finishing in colour.

Alfie Bass (1916–87) was the youngest of ten children born in Gibraltar Walk, Bethnal Green, to a cabinet-maker and his wife. Apart from the war years, he spent his life in acting, starting in the local boys' clubs. He was most famous for his television work, especially his role of Boots in *The Army Game* in the 1950s, but he also made over thirty films.

Angela Lansbury was born in Poplar in 1925, her father and grandfather (Mayor of Poplar) well known in local political circles. She was nominated for an Academy Award for her very first film – *Gaslight*, in 1944 – and is renowned for her versatility from *Bedknobs and Broomsticks* to *Death on the Nile* and *Sweeney Todd*.

Alfred – or Alfie – Lynch died in 2003, aged 72. He was the son of a Whitechapel plumber, born just at the right time for newly recognised working class actors – in *Look Back in Anger*, for instance. He had a busy filming schedule in the 1950s and '60s, from *The Hill* to *The Taming of the Shrew*, and did a lot of television work in the '70s through to the '80s, appearing in everything from *Dr Who* to *Bergerac* to *Lovejoy*.

Georgia Brown (1933–92) was born Lillie Klot in Whitechapel. Her education was via the Brady Girls' Club (for the children of 'impoverished' East End Jews) and the Central Foundation Grammar School, although she spent the years of the Blitz in the safety of Wales. By 1950, she was performing in the West End at The Stork Club, taking her name from one of her cabaret songs: 'Sweet Georgia Brown'.

Bernard Bresslaw (1934–93) was born in the East End to a tailor's cutter father and seamstress mother. He was an active member of the drama society at Cooper's Company School near his home at 73 Eric Street (Bow), lauded for his performance as Long John Silver in *Treasure Island*, and winning many awards for recitation. Not surprisingly, therefore, he did well at RADA and went on to become famous for his television role in *The Army Game* in the 1950s. Although he appeared in fourteen *Carry On* films, he was, less predictably, a Shakespearian actor who was long associated with the Regent's Park Open Air Theatre in central London – which was where he died, waiting to take part in *The Taming of the Shrew*.

Steven Berkoff (admittedly far more than an actor) was born and bred in Stepney, living in Anthony Street. His father had a tailor's shop in Leman Street, Aldgate, and Steven had a Saturday job (when he was 11) working for the Pen King near Whitechapel station, the man who sold 'the first biros to be seen', or so he proclaimed.

Terence Stamp was born in Bancroft Road Maternity Hospital in 1938, a year later than Berkoff (i.e. according to his autobiography – though most sources give 1939). His family were living in Preston's Road, near the Blackwall Tunnel entrance, but moved soon after to Canal Road, Bow, where he spent the war years 'in heaven'. Stamp was immortalised in The Kinks' 'Waterloo Sunset' as Terry of 'Terry and Julie' (Julie being Julie Christie, his then squeeze).

Barbara Windsor was born in London Hospital in 1937 and lived in Shoreditch until 1939 but then she moved out of the East End into Stoke Newington (in North London).

Another (ex-) *East Enders* star is Anita Dobson (or Angie Watts), born in Stepney in April 1949. She was dancing at York Hall by the age of five, and was schooled at John Scurr Primary (E1) and Coborn Grammar (E3) featuring in the school productions, but also attending drama classes at Toynbee Hall in Commercial Street.

More recently, *East Enders*' Bianca, Patsy Palmer, was born Julie Harris in May 1972 in Bethnal Green, and brought up on a council estate while attending Haggerston Girls' Secondary School in Hackney.

VERSATILE EAST ENDERS

The East End's answer to Wilfred Owen was Isaac Rosenberg (killed in 1918). Isaac lived with his family in Cable Street and, latterly, Jubilee Street (both Stepney). He was also a talented painter, taking extra art classes at Stepney Green Art School before going on to study at the Slade School of Art. His best known poems are 'Marching', and 'Break of Day in the Trenches'.

Monty Berman and Robert Baker, from Whitechapel, teamed up in the 1960s as writers, directors and producers for film and television.

Apart from their scripts for Hammer films, they had such successes as *The Saint, Danger Man, The Persuaders, Department S, The Adventures of Robin Hood* and *Gideon's Way*.

Lew Grade and his brother Bernard Delfont (born Winogradsky in Russia before the family emigrated to the East End) were both educated at the Rochelle Street School in Shoreditch and both started in the entertainment world as dancers before the Second World War. Lew Grade was the 1926 World Solo Charleston champion, as judged by Fred Astaire! As Lord Grade and Baron Delfont ('of Stepney'), they ended up as two of the UK's most successful entertainment moguls with great skill at spotting what did and didn't make the 'grade' in television, film and theatre.

Sir Charles Clore, born in 1904 in Casson Street, Mile End, became one of Britain's richest entrepreneurs, worth some £30,000,000. He was behind such High Street names as William Hill, Dolcis, Mappin & Webb and Selfridges, but reputedly started out with the help of £1,000 from his father, a tailor.

Vidal Sassoon, world-renowned coiffeur, grew up in a tenement in Petticoat Lane before the Second World War, and learnt his initial skills from Adolph Cohen who had a hairdressing salon in Whitechapel Road. He became involved in the Jewish paramilitary before achieving fame and fortune in the 1960s, and still, in the USA, is a passionate voice against anti-Semitism.

From Eccentrics . . .

Solomon Eccles, who lived in Spitalfields for most of his life, was an early naturist – of sorts. As a tempestuous Quaker, he was known to have paraded at such places as the Rosemary Fairs and at Westminster

Hall adorned in no more than a fig leaf, bearing a bowl of fire and brimstone on his head and crying 'Repent! Repent!' One naked appearance in Cork in 1670 led to flogging and imprisonment, but he continued to denounce non-believers until his death at Spitalfields in 1682.

Balthazar Gerbier inherited a house in Bethnal Green from his father-in-law in 1646 and decided to open an academy for young gentlemen. Because of the curriculum – languages, military fortifications, horsemanship, navigation and fireworks – this was effectively a useful training ground for would-be spies. It closed in August 1650, with no record of the number of budding James Bonds who graduated.

When Roger Crab was discharged from Cromwell's New Model Army, following a blow on the head, he sold his business as a hatter and gave his money to the poor, ending up as a recluse in the then village of Bethnal Green. It seems that he managed to survive on less than one penny a week, eating grass, dock leaves and mallow. In spite of this, he lived to be 79 – and is rumoured to have been the inspiration, centuries later, for the Mad Hatter in *Alice in Wonderland*.

Arriving in London in 1742, the Jewish mystic Baal Shem (or Dr Falcon) lived in Wellclose Square, Stepney, where he was visited by such believers as the King of Corsica. His books 'of mystery' were apparently insured for £3,000 although he is said to have buried his gold. Baal Shem wore a long robe and a golden turban when sitting on his throne to give 'audiences' and was seen driving his coach at high speed along Mile End Road with his long white hair whirling around him.

During the age of Victorian quack doctors, the Great Sequah frequented the Mile End 'Waste' (Whitechapel market). He always carried discarded crutches, suggesting the number of cures he had effected. His medicines were recommended for everything from cirrhosis of the liver to housemaid's knee. Most famously, however, were his 'painless' teeth extractions. He carried on talking throughout the process, and at the moment when the final pull came, his accompanying brass band (!) produced such a blast of sound that it drowned out any possible screams, proving the painlessness of his treatment.

Thomas Brooks lived in Brick Lane and worked as a chimney sweep from the age of 12. After becoming elected Mayor of Bethnal Green in 1931, he was invited to attend Buckingham Palace for a garden party. Although he agreed to attend, he swept chimneys in the morning and returned to work again at the end of the party – presumably stopping off before the party to clean up.

. . . To Adventurers

When young Walter Raleigh returned to England after fighting in the French civil wars in about 1570, he settled in Blackwall. But before that, he set sail for Guyana from Limehouse in 1546 after his ship had been equipped. A manor house, reputed to have been his home, was demolished in 1890 to make way for the Blackwall Tunnel.

Horatio Nelson is also said to have had a property at Blackwall (possibly the building now known as Nelson's House), handy for his trysts with Lady Hamilton at the Gun.

In 1576, Ratcliff explorer Sir Martin Frobisher left Ratcliff Cross Stairs seeking the North-West Passage. He ended up in Labrador, and came home with two interesting finds: an Eskimo who soon, sadly, died (of heartbreak – or from the English weather?) and some lumps of 'gold', the latter turning out to be worthless. Nevertheless, he returned several times, bringing back some 800 tons in all. His fool's gold ended up as street paving – but he redeemed himself with service against the Spanish Armada, for which he was knighted.

William Burrough/Borough (later Sir) moved to Limehouse from Devon in or before 1579, and was second-in-command to Sir Francis Drake at Cadiz in 1587. Burrough became Comptroller of the Queen's Navy and was responsible for the capture of many pirates, some of whom were executed at Wapping. Although he was indicted for mutiny at one point himself, he was subsequently acquitted. William married Joan Wentworth at St Dunstan's in 1589 and died in Stepney nine years later, buried, predictably, at this same 'naval' church. (Another local man known to Drake was Captain William Cox of Limehouse, who was one of the few Englishmen killed at the battle of the Spanish Armada – while trying to board an enemy vessel.)

William Adams progressed from life as a shipbuilding apprentice in Limehouse to being captain of the *Richard Duffield*, the food and ammunition ship which was a part of the fleet in conflict with the Spanish Armada. In 1600, he was the first Englishman to visit Japan as part of the Dutch East India voyages – although, as it seems he was shipwrecked there, this may not have been his original destination. He became the right-hand-man to Shogun Tokugawa Ieyasu and was, as a result, elevated to becoming the first and only non-Japanese samurai. Adams settled in the country, marrying a Japanese woman but sending money home to his English family, having married Mary at St Dunstan's in 1589. Adams was the inspiration for the book, and film, *Shogun*.

'Honour and Glory' Griffiths from Stepney was the captain of a sloop (*Tryal*) captured by a French man-of-war in 1690. Richard Griffiths and his 'boy' subdued all five Frenchmen who had forced their way on board and delivered them – and their vessel – to safety at Falmouth. He acquired his name from his habit of addressing letters to 'Their honours and glories' (at the Admiralty).

Mariner Isham Randolph married Jane Rogers from Shadwell in 1717. They lived in Shakespeare's Walk, Shadwell, where their daughter, also Jane, was born a few years later (baptised at St Paul's Church, Shadwell) but soon after the whole family moved to Virginia, calling the family plantation Shadwell. It was Jane Randolph Junior who married Peter Jefferson, producing ten children including Thomas, the US President from 1801–9, the man behind the Declaration of Independence.

Captain James Cook moved with his family to the Docklands area at 18 years of age (1746) to work for a ship owner before joining the Navy. He had several different addresses in the East End over the next twenty years (including Assembly Passage and Mile End Road – then under different names), but didn't actually spend much time there as he was far too busy voyaging around Australia, the Antarctic and the Pacific. Having said that, his wife Elizabeth – whose parents ran the Bell at Wapping, from whose unsavoury environs he rescued her (ahhh) – did manage to produce six children. Cook employed a number of local men for his expedition to Australia on the *Endeavour* (1768–71) – including William Peckover, a gunner, and Zachariah Hicks, the first to sight land, both from Wapping.

Captain William Bligh (who was with Cook when the latter was attacked and killed) and Fletcher Christian are supposed to have quenched their thirst at the Town of Ramsgate, Wapping, before sailing on the *Bounty*. Bligh had moved to Broad Street, Wapping (now Reardon Street), with his family in 1785.

Joseph Druce from Shadwell was transported to New South Wales in 1792 for housebreaking and stealing. He met a Maori chief who became ill but Druce was luckily able to nurse him back to health. After marrying one of the chief's daughters (meaning he too was a Maori chief) and having a daughter, he was widowed and returned to Shadwell, spending time in the local workhouse.

General Morris Cohen grew up in Umberston Street, Stepney, and attended the Jews' Free School in Spitalfields. At the turn of the twentieth century, Cohen was sent to reform school (for picking pockets) and then sent to Canada. After the First World War, he returned to his old tricks (in Canada) but became a hero when he went to the aid of the Chinese owner of a gambling house during an armed robbery. Becoming interested in the world of his new Chinese chums, he set off for China and signed up as a bodyguard for Dr Sun Yat-Sen. As a result of the two pistols he always carried, he became a general in the Chinese army known as Two Gun Cohen.

And Not Forgetting The Fairer Sex

Known as the Stepney Amazon, Phoebe Hessel (born in Stepney in about 1713 as Phoebe Smith), followed Samuel Golding, the man she loved, into the Army, disguised as a man. She was just fifteen at the time and it seems that she went on to serve for several years in the West Indies and Gibraltar until she was wounded by a bayonet. The treatment she needed meant she could no longer conceal her sex, and she was discharged. She may or may not have married Golding but she certainly married William Hessel, and lived to the grand old age of 107, her adventures obviously having done her no harm.

When Eliza Marchpane was born into poverty in Stepney in 1760, it was predictable that she join countless other cockney prostitutes in the area. But Eliza was an exception to the rule. She saved, bought her passage to Europe, and called herself the Marquesa de Marchpane. Her accent now came across as more exotic than common and she became a famed courtesan with famous lovers, Mozart among them. When she returned to London, she certainly did not return to Stepney but set up home in the West End importing her favourite French delicacies made from almond paste which became known as 'marchpane' . . . or, you guessed it, marzipan.

Sylvia Pankhurst established the local branch of the Women's Social & Political Union in a disused baker's shop in Bow Road in 1912, and founded the East London Federation of Suffragettes in 1913. This was the year she led a deputation of East Enders to London, resulting in her imprisonment, and she was imprisoned again on several more occasions, spending time in Holloway Prison, often on hunger strike. By 1923, her headquarters had moved to Old Ford Road and she lived in the area for at least one more year. Her pacifist ideals, incidentally, were not necessarily shared by East Enders, men and women, who wanted to defeat the Germans rather than negotiate a peace with them.

SOME FAMOUS PEOPLE WHO DIED IN THE EAST END

Dr James Parkinson, who gave his name to the disease he discovered, originally called the Shaking Palsy, died in Pleasant Row, Hoxton, on 21 December 1824. Hoxton-born, he had trained at the London Hospital and had been the medical attendant to the 'private madhouse' at Holly House, Hoxton.

The Elephant Man, Joseph Merrick, died in the London Hospital in April 1890. He had been given his own room there four years earlier after being discovered by Dr Frederick Treves as an exhibit at 123 Whitechapel Road opposite the London Hospital. Merrick had seen this kind of 'work' as his only alternative to the workhouse but Dr Treves effectively rescued him, writing about the disease which caused his disability (neurofibromatosis) and raising money to fund his care.

David Lean, the film director, spent his final years in Narrow Street, Limehouse, where he died in 1991. The four derelict warehouses he had bought at Sun Wharf had cost him £6,000,000 to convert into his last home.

A Few Unexpected East Enders

William Penn, the founder of Philadelphia and 'all American' hero, was treated rather differently before leaving these shores. As a Quaker, he attended meetings in Spitalfields, and was often in trouble with the law because of his outspoken views, and in further trouble because he refused to remove his hat in court (a Quaker idiosyncrasy). As a result, he spent a few spells in the Tower of London.

The designer of some of the most famous seaside piers (Blackpool North, Brighton West, Margate, Eastbourne, Hastings, Weston-super-Mare and Bournemouth) was an East Ender. Namely Eugenius Birch from Shoreditch, born in 1818, a long way from the sea.

Dr Elizabeth Garrett Anderson, born in Commercial Road in 1836, was the first woman in England to qualify in medicine, the first to obtain a degree at the Sorbonne, founder of the first hospital to be staffed by women for women (then in Marylebone Road, central London), and the first woman Mayor in England (at Aldeburgh in Suffolk). Didn't she do well?

When illiterate Barney Barnato from Whitechapel, grandson of a Rabbi, left for South Africa in 1873 with £50 in his pocket, little did he know that, thanks to his skill in diamond dealing, he would return three years later with £3,000. By 1895, he was reputedly worth £4,000,000! His visiting card said it all: 'I'll stand you a drink, but I won't lend you a fiver'.

The son of a dock labourer, Walter Edwards (born in Whitechapel in 1900) became a stoker in the Royal Navy but made it all the way to the top, becoming the only Civil Lord of the Admiralty with this humble background.

Abraham Beame was born in Whitechapel in 1906 and left these shores early on, with his family, to become the first Jewish Mayor of New York City. When his period in office finished he had turned the city round from near bankruptcy to a huge ($200,000,000) surplus. New York, your debt is to Whitechapel.

THE POLITICALLY CORRECT?

In 1895, Mancherjee Merwanjee Bhownaggree, born in Bombay, won the Tory seat for Bethnal Green North East and remained their MP until 1906. He was the first Asian Tory MP. Because of his sympathies with Britain's Imperial stance, he became known in some circles as 'Bow and Agree' but was a highly respected figure in political circles.

Percy Harris, the MP for South and West Bethnal Green from 1922 to 1945, won six consecutive elections and was often the only Liberal MP within 100 miles of London.

The first woman elected to represent a London Borough (1923) was Susan Lawrence, who lived just off East India Dock Road for many years. She was one of the first three Labour women MPs, the first woman elected to the LCC (1910), the first Labour woman to address the House of Commons, and the first female Chair of the Labour party. When representing Poplar, she was one of several women imprisoned in September 1921 for contempt of court when protesting about the unfairness of LCC rates.

When Mahatma Gandhi came over for the Round Table Conference (on India) at Whitehall in 1931, he declined the use of a hotel, and chose to stay at Kingsley Hall in Bow, among the working class. He had met Muriel Lester, the visionary behind the settlement, and caused quite a stir locally. The Pearly King and Queen of East London were among the stream of visitors that met him during his twelve-week stay between September and December.

Clement Attlee was Mayor for Stepney and Labour MP for Limehouse before becoming prime minister in 1945 and establishing the NHS and the welfare state. He said that he would take the title of Lord Love-a-duck of Limehouse if elevated to the peerage – in fact, he became Earl of Walthamstow (close).

In 1993, the British National Party secured its first elected representative at Millwall, when Derek Beackon won by just seven votes. Formerly an unemployed lorry driver, his smile faded when Labour took back the seat just nine months later.

SOME POPULATION STATISTICS

Census figures reveal the following variations in changes to the local population from 1801 to 1951:

Poplar went up hugely from 8,278 to 73,544
Stepney went down from 113,281 to 98,858
Bethnal Green went up from 22,310 to 58,374

Workhouse records for 1888 reveal (estimated?) numbers of 'official' paupers:

Whitechapel	1,503
St George's	1,164
Poplar	3,956
Mile End	1,842

The 1901 census reveals that 42,032 Russians and Poles were living in Stepney. By 1990, there were 10,000 Somalians in Tower Hamlets (following civil war), and by 2001 the emphasis had shifted again: there were 6,000 Bangladeshis in Whitechapel alone, over 50 per cent of the population. (Note that Tower Hamlets Council now uses Banglatown as an official description of the area around Brick Lane.)

2001 census figures for the area:

Bethnal Green	37,125
Blackwall	11,939
Bow	19,218
Bromley-by-Bow	11,581
Limehouse	23,980
Mile End	22,940
Millwall	12,892
Shadwell	12,078
Spitalfields	8,383
Stepney	12,679
Wapping	11,245
Whitechapel	12,046

6

PLACES

Saved And Listed: Some Unusual Examples

The Grade II listed building which once housed the dockmaster's house for Limehouse Basin is now a gastro-pub run by Gordon Ramsay (The Narrow, in Narrow Street).

Although William Cubitt's sailmaking and ship-chandlers business, which opened in Commercial Road, Bow, in 1869, did not survive – along with similar businesses that had relied on the shipping industry – the building/workshop (later taken over by Caird & Rayner) was Grade II listed in 2000, and is now owned by the Peabody Trust.

The railway viaduct over the London and Blackwall Railway (which crosses Limehouse basin) is Grade II listed.

A row of shops in Raven Row, Artillery Lane, Spitalfields, once the home of Huguenot silk merchants, is now Grade I listed and used as an arts centre.

Trinity Green Almshouses, Mile End Road, complete with railings, are Grade I listed. They are the work of Sir Christopher Wren, dating from 1695, on land provided by Captain Henry Mudd (from Ratcliff) for 'twenty-eight decayed masters and commanders of ships' or their widows.

From 1890 to 1977, the London Hydraulic Company on Wapping Wall operated under the label of the 'world's oldest hydraulic station'. The quiet and powerful nature of hydraulics meant that this company powered the lifting engines of Tower Bridge, the safety curtains at West End theatres including the London Palladium, and the movable dance floor at the Savoy. The building remains as a gallery and eaterie, the last fully-fitted building of its type in Britain. Retaining many original features, it is Grade II listed.

The Soup Kitchen for the Jewish Poor in Brune Street, Spitalfields, last of many in the area, has a Grade II listed façade – although the interior is now smart apartments and offices.

Three cast-iron lamp standards on the pavement outside 805 Commercial Road are Grade II listed.

Kingsley Hall in Powis Road, Bow, was Grade II listed in 1973 – an Arts and Crafts Building built in 1928 as a hostel and community centre at the instigation of Doris and Muriel Lester (the latter a peace campaigner and writer).

The Troxy in Commercial Road, Stepney, has been a cinema, a wartime air-raid shelter, a dance hall, a bingo hall, theatre and private function hall. Its Art Deco exterior, dating from 1933, is preserved as a result of its Grade II listing.

The eighteenth-century House Mill on Three Mills Lane, Bow, is Grade I listed, and offers guided tours. The nearby Clock Mill is Grade II listed and now houses a film studio; but the third mill – a windmill – is long gone.

Parts of the school-keeper's house at Stepney Jewish School, Stepney Green, (now artists' studios) are Grade II listed, along with part of the old school frontage and the gate piers.

Student accommodation belonging to Queen Mary College (Mile End Road), known as Albert Stern House, was built in 1913 as a home and hospital for local Spanish and Portuguese Jews. It is now Grade II listed.

The gents' toilets outside St Mary's Church (Bow Road) were a surprising addition to the Grade II listings in 2009. Gladstone's nearby statue seems to be pointing at them in admiration.

The Boundary Estate in Shoreditch, the UK's first public housing development, was built in the 1890s on the 15-acre site of a notorious slum (known as Old Nichol or the Jago). Comprising twenty-three tower blocks, it is now Grade II listed. Arnold Circus forms the centre of the estate, with its bandstand, used for community events.

Tobacco Dock, Porters Walk, Wapping, is a Grade I listed warehouse dating from 1812 with unique cast-iron roof trusses. It is now a desolate structure, used since 2008 for the colourful annual London Tattoo Convention. Although a long way from the original brief for this Victorian building, at least this event brings back swarms of people (some 20,000) for a while to a building that was once full of traders, warehousemen and seamen dealing in tobacco.

The Grade II listed People's Palace (now part of Queen Mary and Westfield College), Mile End Road, was designed to alleviate local boredom and poverty, and offering more than entertainment: it offered hands-on training in a range of skills. It was opened by George VI.

Within Victoria Park (itself a Conservation Area since 1977) are two eighteenth-century stone alcoves – on its east side – which were originally 'traffic shelters' on the since-replaced London Bridge, and are both Grade II listed. The park's pinnacled Gothic water fountain was a gift from a Victorian philanthropist (Baroness Angela Burdett-Coutts), and is similarly listed.

Keeling House, four once-crumbling sixteen-storey towers, created a controversy when it was listed Grade II in 1993 – the first post-war building and first council block to receive this honour. It is in Claredale Street, Bethnal Green, and is now private housing, with one-bedroom 'apartments' changing hands at around £250,000. Sir Denys Lasdun, the designer, was also responsible for such gems as the National Theatre in London. (Twenty-six-storey Balfron Tower in Poplar was similarly listed in 1996).

Hospital Hot Spots

St Katharine's Hospital (for the poor) was founded in 1147 by Queen Matilda on the site of what is now St Katharine's Dock – although destroyed during the redevelopment, it resurfaced as a retreat in Butcher Row, Ratcliff, just off Commercial Road.

In 1197, the New Hospital of St Mary Without Bishopsgate started life in what is now Spitalfields. It was one of the largest hospitals in medieval England (and the largest in the London area), becoming St Mary Spital before Henry VIII removed it (and the attached Augustinian priory) in 1539 during the Dissolution. The remains of its fourteenth-century charnel house, one of only four in England (for the storage of bones disturbed by burials) can be seen through the modern office windows of Allen & Overy, Bishops Square, Spitalfields. The Society for the Protection of Ancient Buildings in Spital Square is on the site of the original hospital which has also been the site (*c.* 1740) of a silk merchant's house.

The Magdalen Hospital for the Reception of Penitent Prostitutes provided a retreat for those in distress and was established in Prescot Street, Whitechapel, in 1758 (later – much later – to become the first street in London with numbered housing). After some twelve years, it moved to large premises in South London, the building now long demolished.

An infirmary started in 1741 in Prescot Street led to the London Hospital which was established in 1753. By 1876 it was the largest in the country with 790 beds. It was also the location for the first hospital-based medical school in England (1785) and probably the first radiograph image (of a needle in a foot) in 1896. It was at the London Hospital that war heroine Edith Cavell received her nursing training – from 1896. She went on to become the assistant matron at Shoreditch Infirmary in 1903. The first successful operation to stretch the mitral valve, the basis for modern heart surgery, was performed by Sir Henry Souttar at 'The London' in 1925. More recently, Fred Pontin (of holiday camp fame) financed a new operating theatre here in 1957 after being successfully treated following a serious car accident. In 1990, it became the Royal London Hospital after a visit from the queen, the same year that its helipad was opened.

The Poplar Hospital for Accidents was opened in 1858 as the first hospital for dockers, whose injuries were often too serious to allow them the journey to the London Hospital in Mile End Road. It sported a sign in pre-motor-car days which asked 'Drivers – kindly walk past hospital' to show consideration for patients. Such courtesy did not save it, because it closed in 1975.

During the cholera outbreak in London in the mid-nineteenth century, the Admiralty made HMS *Dover* available as a floating hospital, which was moored first off Limehouse and then off Hermitage Pier, Wapping. In spite of this, and the Wapping District Cholera Emergency Hospital, some 4,000 East Londoners died as a result of contracting the disease.

The original East London Hospital for Children and Dispensary for Women was founded by Nathaniel and Sarah Heckford in 1868 in an old warehouse in Butcher Row, Ratcliff, and was visited by Charles Dickens. The author's recommendations brought in additional funding, and a bigger building was constructed in Glamis Road, Shadwell, in 1877 (opened by the Duchess of Teck) with Dr Elizabeth Garrett Anderson as the Medical Officer. It was the first London hospital for children under two years of age, changing its name to the Princess Elizabeth of York Hospital for Children (1932) and merging with the Queen Elizabeth Hospital for Children (in Hackney) ten years later, the latter closing in 1963.

The London Chest Hospital in Bethnal Green was one of the first hospitals to care for tuberculosis patients in London (established 1848). In 2009, it became the pioneer for a state-of-the-art chest

scanner, the first in the UK, able to pinpoint previously undetectable heart problems – costing £1,000,000.

Her Majesty's Hospital in Stepney Causeway (from 1888) was the largest children's hospital in London at that time. The adjacent buildings, numbers 18 to 26, were leased by Dr Barnardo, the expansion completed over seven years resulting in space for 253 children. By 1899, Dr Barnardo had taken over the hospital and every building on one side of Stepney Causeway, adding houses in Bower Street soon after to suit his ever-growing requirements. The children were evacuated in 1939, and never returned – Barnardo's found alternative premises outside London (although a presence was maintained in Stepney Causeway until as recently as 1969).

St Clement's Hospital in Bow Road was originally the City of London Union Workhouse (the hospital closed in 2005).

LOST HISTORIES

Bromley Hall in Brunswick Road, Bow, is arguably the oldest brick-built house in London, originally dating back to 1490, with even older foundations. During its long life, it has been a manor house, a hunting lodge, a gunpowder factory (during the Civil War), a calico printing works, and a carpet warehouse – more recently restored for office units.

A mansion called Bednall House dating from 1570, known as (John) Kirby's Castle, was turned into a lunatic asylum in 1727 and had 542 inmates by 1841. It was rebuilt in 1843, and, during the First World War, was used to house German prisoners. Although the building was demolished in the 1920s to make way for a housing estate, the local park (where Bethnal Green Library stands) is still known as Barmy Park.

400 Old Ford Road was the former HQ of the East London Federation of Suffragettes, and later the People's Russian Information Bureau (following the Russian Revolution of 1917). It has since been demolished.

Bow Road has a particularly political history: it was the home of MP George Lansbury's election headquarters (the man who told PM Asquith that he would go down in history as a man who tortured innocent women, i.e. the suffragettes), of the Women's Social & Political Union, the National Union of Women's Suffrage Societies, the Votes for Women Fellowship, the Men's Political Union for Women's Emancipation, the National League for Opposing Women's Suffrage and the Unionist committee rooms.

LOST STREETS

Cock Lane, Rogues Lane and Whores Lane all disappeared with the coming of Old Bethnal Green Road – now a conservation area.

Cat's Hole, Pillory Lane and Dark Entry were dodgy streets swept away by the development of St Katharine's Dock – as this was in 1825, it sounds like the earliest example of slum clearance in the area.

Ducking Pond Row, Whitechapel, (with nearby ducking pond) was no doubt a handy place to deal with witches – or drunks.

A court known as the Land of Promise disappeared around the same time as the nearby Shoreditch Workhouse (it was off what is now Catherine Wheel Alley).

In Bow, one street has changed from Beareburden Lane (bearbind a form of convolvulvus) to Beerbinder Lane to Tredegar Road, named after landowner Sir Charles Morgan of Tredegar – but Berebinder House remains on the corner.

SOME DIVERSE ROOTS

The Isle of Dogs has a whole range of explanations for its name, dating back to 1588, prior to which it was Stepney Marsh. It could have been the site of Henry VIII's (among others) kennels, or a derivation from the 'dykes' built in the area in the nineteenth century, or a misnomer of 'Isle of Ducks' or because of the large number of canine corpses washed up by the tide (according to *The Graphic* of 23 February 1889). There is even a story of its origins in the murder of a man whose dog swam back and forth to Greenwich until someone discovered the body and the murderer was detected, again according to *The Graphic*. Incidentally, it seems that in the seventeenth century, the Isle of Dogs had just two inhabitants, the man who drove the cattle off the marshes and the man who operated the ferry to Greenwich.

Poplar originates in the large number of poplar trees once thriving, and similarly Bromley-by-Bow is popularly thought to derive from 'bramble'. Bow is from the bow-shaped bridge which Will Kempe (a Shakespearean actor) was said to cross on his nine-day Morris dance from Stepney to Norwich in 1600 – the nine days' wonder.

Stem is strap-shaped – *flat* and flaccid. This makes it catch the wind – and so the leaf *trembles*.

POPLAR

Spitalfields is a contraction of Hospital Fields, and the name Shadwell derives from Chadwelle (a mineral spring dedicated to St Chad) or shallow well.

Millwall comes from the windmills for grinding corn once existing on the Isle of Dogs. Blackwall is probably from the moss-covered wall originally built to hold back flood damage – which was, er, black.

Stepney has a plethora of explanations – perhaps the landing place of Stebba, Styba or Stephen, or the home of Stebba's people. Similarly, Bethnal Green is seemingly from Blida's Corner (all Saxon names).

Wapping is said to be the home of Waeppa's people or, arguably, from 'wapol' – the Old English for marsh. Limehouse is named after its lime-kilns.

Whitechapel dates from a white chapel of *c.* 1270 (later St Mary Matfelon Church or St Mary's, demolished after Second World War damage). The site is now Altab Ali Park, named after the young man murdered in a racial attack in 1978, with a Bengali poem embedded in its path.

Streets Have Roots Too

Knighten Street, off Wapping High Street, owes its name to a guild of thirteen knights who were in control of what was then a rough area outside the London walls in the tenth century.

Frying Pan Alley gets its name from the ironmongers and braziers who used to hang frying pans outside their shops.

Brick Lane derives from its earlier function as a route for the bricks being carried from brick kilns in Spitalfields. In the sixteenth century, brick-makers were housed in the street, the land being suited to the trade.

Petticoat Lane is actually Middlesex Street, its name changed because the reference to 'petticoats' (linked to earlier Huguenot lace-makers) was not popular with the Victorians.

Gun Street, Spitalfields, is said to follow the line of the gunnery within the old artillery ground utilised by Henry VIII's Artillery Company (hence also Artillery Lane and Artillery Passage).

Canary Wharf is not named after the bird, but the islands from which tomatoes were imported. Similarly, Shoulder of Mutton Alley in Limehouse owes its origins to the days of meat being unloaded in huge quantities at local docks. A modern development here extends the derivation – it is called Lamb Court.

Thermopylae Gate on the Chapel House Estate (built on the Isle of Dogs in the 1920s and 1930s as 'Homes for Heroes' of the First World War) is named after a nineteenth-century clipper, as is Hesperus Crescent. Macquarie Way was named after the last known clipper to return home to Poplar, and the maritime theme continues in the area.

A different theme in Limehouse: streets called Ming, Nankin, Canton and Pekin . . . the Chinatown connection lingers on.

Poplar's themed streets (in an area once known as Bromley Marsh) originate from the one-time owner of the land, Hugh McIntosh from the East India Company. His grandson sold some of the land in 1873 as developments started taking over from the rural landscape, but its Scottish roots continue in Culloden Street, Lochnagar Street, Oban Street and Zetland Street (the archaic spelling of Shetland).

EIGHT INTERESTING EAST END MUSEUMS

The area's oldest museum is the Grade II listed Bethnal Green Museum, an offshoot of the Victoria & Albert, opened in 1872 using an iron structure which had been built for the Great Exhibition of 1851. It was the first home for the renowned Wallace Collection and is now known as the V&A Museum of Childhood, specialising in childhood objects – with the largest collection in the UK. In recent years it has boasted a display of sixteenth-century swaddling bands and a seventeenth-century nappy, the oldest in any public collection (and presumably unsullied). Moving right along, the museum paid £25,000 in 2006 for the oldest rocking horse in the UK (*c.* 1605–8), thought to have belonged to Charles I, a happier evocation of childhood in softwood and elm.

The Geffrye Museum in Kingsland Road, Shoreditch, on the very edge of the East End, is where you can walk through time, through a series of period rooms from the sixteenth to the twentieth centuries. The building is in a converted eighteenth-century almshouse, surrounded by five period gardens and an award-winning herb garden featuring 170 herbs. The gardens were designed by Fanny Wilkinson, the Charlie Dimmock of her age, when the museum was a series of almshouses for local ironmongers.

The Royal London Hospital Museum is housed in the crypt of a nineteenth-century Gothic church (St Philip's) in Newark Street, Whitechapel.

The Museum of Immigration and Diversity in Princelet Street combines a master silk weaver's house (dating from 1719) with a Victorian synagogue (1869) – the only listed building in Britain (Grade II) with its particular specialisations.

Opened in 1990, the Ragged School Museum in Copperfield Road, Bow, utilises the only mid-Victorian canalside warehouses left in the area. Some of these buildings were originally rented by Dr Barnardo for a Ragged School (free for poor children) which, by 1879, was the largest 'ragged' day school of the 144 in London.

The Museum of London Docklands, dating from 2003, is at West India Quay in a Grade I listed Georgian sugar warehouse. The massive timber and stone structure houses twelve galleries of artefacts and was the largest museum to open in London for over twenty years.

The Thames River Police Museum in Wapping High Street details the history of this country's first ever police force. Visits are by appointment because it is part of a working police station, and the curator is a police officer.

Dennis Severs' House in Folgate Street, Spitalfields, recreates the fictional story of a family of silk weavers in this eighteenth-century time capsule. Tours are conducted in silence, with the rooms as if the family had just popped out.

East End Markets

Spitalfields Market is believed to date back to the thirteenth century when it was held in a field, but a Royal Charter of the seventeenth century meant that the site of Spital Square could be used. It became an expanding centre for the supply of fresh fruit, vegetables and flowers, and grew at such a rate that it finally had to move to Leyton (E10) at the end of the 1980s. The Victorian market building and its surrounds now house the New Spitalfield Market, offering a much wider variety of goods.

There was a hugely popular hay market in Whitechapel until 1928. The market moved there from a smaller site in Ratcliff dating back to 1708. The rural sight of carts laden with hay was a regular sight along the wide Whitechapel Road. Nowadays, Whitechapel Market is a conservation area (since 1997) with more than eighty stalls, and is part of a flagship plan which means that 100 per cent of its waste is recycled – 9 tons every week.

Columbia Market in Bethnal Green was a short-lived covered market, an expensive venture. The £20,000 bill was picked up by the richest woman in England: philanthropist Angela Burdett-Coutts, from the Coutts banking dynasty. It opened in 1869 but could not compete with the street markets that the rather suspicious East Enders were used to. Although it closed in 1886, its cellars were used in the Second World War as an air-raid shelter but proved unfit for this purpose, and the building was demolished in 1960.

Roman Road Market is situated on the oldest known trade route in Britain. Archways at each end, inscribed in Latin to reflect this Roman heritage, appeared in 1986 and the whole area is a conservation area.

Petticoat Lane (a previous name along with Bereward's Lane and Hog Lane, but real name Middlesex Street) may have been the Victorian home of soup kitchens, the Jewish Free School and the Salvation Army, but by the twentieth century had become a tourist attraction because of its market. Sunday trading took place here before it was 'legalised' in 1936 because the majority of traders were Jewish, their Sabbath being on Saturday. While the ethnicity may have changed in more recent years, the name, and the market, live on.

Signs Of The Times

By the 1970s, the Borough of Tower Hamlets had more tower blocks (eight storeys or higher) than any other part of London – nearly 100.

The tallest building in the UK at 235m – at least until 2012 – is no. 1 Canada Square on the Isle of Dogs (Canary Wharf), known as the Canary Wharf Tower. The second and third tallest are close by at no. 8 and no. 25 Canada Square.

On 1 March 1970, after the docks had started closing, the Isle of Dogs declared independence from the UK, as a protest against a lack of facilities for the islanders. 'President' Ted Johns (a Labour councillor) and his cohorts erected border posts at Limehouse and the Blackwall Tunnel. A cunning plan, it was not taken too seriously and crumbled within days from lack of support.

7

BATTLES & WARS, RIOTS & STRIKES

NOTHING LIKE A GOOD RIOT

1381

The leaders of the Peasants' Revolt, Wat Tyler and John Ball, met 14-year-old Richard II at Mile End on 14 June. Between 20,000 and 60,000 rebels from Kent and Essex (agricultural workers, tradesmen and soldiers) were protesting about yet another proposed poll tax, and this location was a kind of halfway house outside the city walls. It was the first major rebellion by the populace in British history, and the promises King Richard II made to end feudalism met the fate of the promises of many teenagers – unfulfilled.

1450

Jack Cade headed an assembly of thousands of men from Kent, Essex, Surrey, Sussex and Middlesex on Mile End Green – a popular meeting spot for rebels, obviously – after they had occupied London to protest about the insolvent and corrupt court of King Henry VI. This was the Kentish Revolt, which ended in Jack Cade's defeat – and death – after a battle on London Bridge.

1517

The year of the Evil May Day Riots when foreign-owned property was attacked, resulting in the deaths of 135 Flemings in Stepney.

1666

Hundreds of Wapping (and other) seamen tried to rescue comrades from prisons and had to be quelled by force in spite of what Samuel Pepys wrote of as their 'just clamour' over poor pay and working conditions.

1719

The Calico Riots saw 4,000 Spitalfields weavers controlled by troops after their attacks on anyone wearing imported Indian calico, which deprived the weavers of their livelihood.

1736

Anti-Irish riots exploded during the rebuilding of St Leonard's Church in Shoreditch, when English workmen were sacked and replaced with lower paid Irish labourers. 'Irish' establishments such as the Queen's Head, the White Hart and the Gentleman & Porter were all demolished, with cries of 'Down with the wild Irish!' Five rioters were imprisoned.

1769

The Spitalfield Riots followed the decline of the silk industry with weavers setting up a funding system for those out of work – frowned upon by employers who took it as a means of forcing up wages. A party of soldiers, encountering with resistance at a meeting of weavers in the Dolphin (probably in Artillery Lane), opened fire and arrested several rioters. John Doyle and John Valline (Irish and French origins respectively) were hanged in front of the Salmon & Ball in Bethnal Green in December 1769. The men claimed to have been framed, and the angry crowd pulled down the gibbet after they were hanged.

1780

The Gordon Riots began with the burning of two Catholic chapels in Stepney (one of them part of a hospital for foreign sailors in Lukin Street) and the homes of Catholics in Poplar and Spitalfields. The Protestant mobs objected to the reduction of restrictions against Catholics, and were on their way to Downing Street – although many did not get farther than the breweries and pubs en route. As many as 12,000 troops were deployed to deal with the problem, which resulted in 700 deaths – although the number who died from alcohol poisoning is not recorded.

1882

The Skeleton Army pelted Salvationists in Bethnal Green with flour, eggs and stones. They were against the Salvation Army message, carrying banners with the skull and crossbones, and even coffins. The Bethnal Green riots, initiated by what the press described as a 'rabble' of 'vagabonds', led to similar troubles all over London.

1919

Cable Street became the scene of a riot against mixed-race relationships, with gunshots fired and a café destroyed.

DIFFERENT KINDS OF BATTLE

A fleet of forty-seven ships arrived at Blackwall in 1471, led by Thomas 'The Bastard' Neville (Lord Fauconberg) who was intending to snatch King Henry VI from protective custody at the Tower of London. The rescuers only got as far as Aldgate, where they were forced to retreat, through Mile End, Blackwall, and over the river to Kent. Fauconberg failed in his attempt and was caught and executed, surviving Henry himself by just a few months.

Royalist insurgents seized Bow Bridge in June 1648 during the Civil War. Although they captured the turnpike, they were attacked by parliamentary forces and retreated to Colchester.

In October 1798, two coal-heavers and a watchman's boy were fined for stealing coal at the Thames Magistrates' Court attached to the new Marine Police Office at Wapping. The fines were considered wholly inappropriate by the hostile crowd collecting outside, and as many as 2,000 attempted to burn down the police station with the officers inside, after one had shot a 'rioter'. This was actually Gabriel Franks, a master lumper (responsible for unloading cargoes from vessels protected by the Marine Police Office and thus a part of the police force) who was seeking a cutlass to protect the officers. He died a few days later in London Hospital and was, thus, the first English policeman to be killed in the line of duty. Although it proved impossible to attribute the shot to anyone in particular, James Eyers was convicted because of his actions in starting the riot, and he was hanged.

Stepney was the site of violence in October 1813 between some 500 members of two Chinese 'clans', the Chenies and the Chin-Choo. A knife-wielding battle took place at the East India Company's barracks in Shadwell resulting in three deaths and seventeen wounded, although the fight had started over an unpaid debt of just 1*s* 6*d*.

The Battle of Stepney, otherwise known as the Siege of Sidney Street, followed a bungled jewel heist in Houndsditch in December 1910. Three policemen were killed during the burglary attempt, and the police were tipped off that the perpetrators – a Latvian immigrant gang – were sheltering in Betty Gershon's upstairs flat at 100 Sidney Street. The two men in the flat had removed Betty's skirt and shoes to prevent her leaving, but the police managed to rescue her from the lower floor when they arrived early on 3 January 1911, but they did not expect the level of resistance they met. The two (possibly three) men resisted arrest by firing Mauser pistols from the upstairs windows, with plenty of witnesses looking on, including Winston Churchill at one point who ended up with a bullet hole in his hat. At least one policeman was injured, and the overwhelmed force was subsequently assisted by twenty-one marksmen from the Scots Guards, until the building burst into flames, with two bodies inside, one killed by a marksman's bullet, one by smoke inhalation. Subsequently, the gang's superior fire power led the London police to improve their own 'armoury'. Interestingly, throughout the eight-hour siege, the postman continued to deliver mail to Sidney Street residents.

On 4 October 1936, the people of the East End prevented Sir Oswald Mosley and some 3,000 'Blackshirts', members of the British Union of

Fascists, from marching through Cable Street in Stepney, then mainly a Jewish area. The greatest East End crowd in living memory massed at Gardiner's Corner (Aldgate), quoted to be as many as 300,000, assisted by abandoned trams and lorries which blocked access roads. Known as the Battle of Cable Street, there was actually little violence, as the BUF were ordered to turn back by the police, although they did take petty revenge a week later by smashing windows in Jewish shops in the Mile End Road.

The Battle of Wapping in 1986 was the result of 6,000 newspaper workers striking when News International moved its workers from Fleet Street to Wapping, without union agreement. Fortress Wapping was besieged in what was an ultimately unsuccessful attempt to thwart the move.

The IRA ended a two-year ceasefire when they bombed South Quay (Canary Wharf) in 1996, killing two people and injuring thirty-nine including three policemen. This was then one of Britain's biggest peace-time bombings, the device having been hidden in a lorry; it caused damage worth £85 million including the demolition of a six-storey office building.

ONE OUT, ALL . . .

Young girls from the East End's nineteenth-century slums suffered further deprivation at the hands of some unscrupulous employers, including Bryant & May, who produced millions of matches in their Fairfield Road factory. Their cause was taken on by Annie Besant, the social reformer who was invited to be their strike leader after writing an article called 'White Slavery in London' in 1888. The girls – some as young as thirteen – were not only paid as little as 4s per week for a ten-hour day (standing all the while) but had deductions made for their equipment or for breaking rules such as leaving a match on a bench. Worse still, many developed 'Phossy jaw' – a disfiguring and painful complaint resulting from their daily exposure to yellow phosphorus. The strike, the first in the history of the Labour movement which involved such a large number of women (figures range from 672 to 1,400), lasted a fortnight, and resulted in better conditions and the foundation of the Matchmakers' Union.

The 1889 Dock Strike (protesting against wages and systems) was distinguished not just by the numbers taking part (as many as 130,000) but also by the nature of the marches from Commercial Road to the City of London. These marches incorporated imaginative tableaux, brass bands, fancy dress, plenty of banners – of course – but mainly avoided violence. The secretary of the Strike Committee was Eleanor Marx, daughter of Karl, working from their HQ in Jeremiah Street, Poplar, and the strike had the support of such local organisations as the Salvation Army in Whitechapel Road, who supplied some 10,000 loaves a day to the strikers. When, after four weeks, the strikers were nearing starvation, they were aided by some £30,000 from their Australian counterparts. Their main demand, for 6*d* an hour (the dockers' tanner) instead of 5*d*, was finally met when such luminaries as the Lord Mayor of London and the Archbishop of Westminster showed support for their cause. This strike became a turning point in the history of trade unionism.

The hunger strikes carried out by the suffragettes before the First World War seem to have started when Sylvia Pankhurst and two of her comrades were sentenced to two months' hard labour in Holloway Prison after hurling a stone through the window of Selby's the undertakers in Bow Road (near Bromley High Street) in 1913. Her colleagues joined in by smashing windows in nearby buildings, with all the women being locked up at Bow police station before moving to Holloway.

In 1914, 300 women employed as tin-makers at Morton's, the Millwall cannery and merchants, went on strike to protest at the low wages being paid to unskilled girls under the age of eighteen, presumably in an attempt to cut wage costs. All 1,000 employees quickly joined in the strike, which was described in an issue of the *Daily Mail* as a strike by 'Tango Dancing Girls' (the headline accompanying a picture of the women dancing in the street to draw attention to their demands). Management held out for just twelve days before acceding to the strikers' requests.

FIRST WORLD WAR, COCKNEY STYLE

A commandeered bus was used as an army recruitment office running from the Poplar Recreation Ground to the Tower of London via East India Dock Road, its destination board declaring 'To Berlin and Back Free'.

The first batch of 100 wounded soldiers to arrive at Waterloo station were taken to the London Hospital, Whitechapel, in taxis and vans loaned by J. Lyons & Co.

The deadliest German raid on London during the First World War resulted in one bomb from a Gotha G dropping on a nursery school in Great North Street, Poplar, during a daylight raid. This caused the death of eighteen 5-year-olds. The date, 13 June 1917, is commemorated on a memorial in Poplar Park, East India Dock Road.

In September 1917, a baker from Chapman Street, Shadwell, was imprisoned for three weeks for selling fresh bread. Only day-old bread was allowed to be sold because it was easier to cut into thin slices and therefore went further at a time of bread shortages.

SECOND WORLD WAR, BUT PLENTY TO SMILE ABOUT

A week after the Blitz, two leading Stepney Communists (Messrs Piratin and Rosen) led 100 East Enders to the Savoy Hotel in the West End to seek shelter and to draw attention to the disparity between the shelters available in the West End and the East End. Sadly, after their long walk, the all-clear sounded, and they didn't get to stay in the lap of luxury, even briefly.

A special branch of Bethnal Green library was opened in the local tube station with a stock of some 4,000 books to serve the 10,000 or so using the station as a shelter. The nearby Bethnal Green Museum was converted into a public restaurant serving 1,000 meals per day at 1s each.

The underground goods yard underneath the railway arch between Leman Street and Commercial Road, known as the Tilbury Shelter, was officially recognised as suitable for up to 3,000 people (in spite of having just two toilets) but was used by as many as 16,000.

The first flying bomb (or V1 or buzz-bomb or doodlebug) to be dropped on London crash-landed in Grove Road, Bow, on 13 June 1944. Local cockneys had quite a surprise when they couldn't find the body of the pilot, until realising that this was a pilotless device.

Gert and Daisy, otherwise known as Bow sisters Elsie and Doris Waters, presented a mobile canteen to Poplar during the war years, and were known to take their turn in pouring tea for 'customers'. They also entertained people sheltering in the underground tube stations with their own brand of comedy and music. Their brother, Horace, better known as Jack Warner (the post-war *Dixon of Dock Green*) took part in *Garrison Theatre*, a radio show for the troops.

THE PRIDE OF THE EAST END

Son of a master mariner, it is no surprise that George Chicken, who lived in King David Lane, Shadwell, followed in his father's footsteps. He served with the Indian Naval Brigade during the Indian Mutiny and was awarded the VC in 1858 for single-handedly fending off an attack by twenty armed mutineers at the Battle of Suhejnee (Bengal), five of whom he killed with his sword before being rescued, although wounded. He was the last volunteer during the mutiny to be so honoured and one of only five civilians. Unfortunately, he went down with his ship, *Emily*, in the Bay of Bengal in 1860 before his VC could be awarded, but it turned up in the hands of Sotheby's in 2006 when it sold for £48,000.

Issy Smith arrived in Wapping as a stowaway, in about 1900, and enrolled himself at Berner Street School (off Commercial Road). As the son of French Jews, he felt relatively comfortable in the area, and served in the British Army from 1904 at the age of fourteen. While in India, Issy (born Ishroulch Shmeilowitz) won the Delhi Durbar Medal – and also became a champion boxer. He was discharged in 1912 and emigrated to Australia before being called up at the outbreak of the First World War. As a result of the outstanding gallantry he displayed at Ypres, carrying the wounded to safety while exposed to heavy fire, he became the first living Jewish recipient of the Victoria Cross, and was also awarded the French *Croix de Guerre*. His VC was sold in 1990 for £30,000 although he had originally pawned it for just £20, only to receive it back thanks to the Chief Rabbi's intervention.

Corporal Alfred Drake was killed in action at La Brique in Belgium in 1915 after saving the lives of others, including his officer, oblivious to enemy attack. He was born in Skidmore Street, Stepney, in December 1893 and served with the 8th Battalion of the Rifle Brigade. His actions merited a posthumous VC and he is also commemorated on one of Gallahers' series of cigarette cards (the Victoria Cross heroes).

Sergeant William Burman, born 1897 in Baker Street, Stepney, another member of the Rifle Brigade, lived to receive his VC. This ex-pupil of Stepney Redcoat School single-handedly seized an enemy machine gun during the battle of Passchendaele at Ypres in September 1917, turning the gun on the enemy, resulting in six enemy dead and thirty-one captured.

Private Sidney Godley, born in about 1889, was the first private soldier during the First World War to be honoured with a Victoria Cross. As a machine gunner with the Royal Fusiliers, he manned one of just two guns facing six German divisions at Mons, successfully defending a railway bridge despite being wounded. Taken prisoner, his captors thought so highly of him that they invited him to join their officers for Christmas dinner! After the war he became the caretaker at Cranbrook Street School in Bethnal Green until his retirement. As an aside, his uncle, George Godley, was one of the police officers involved in the Jack the Ripper case.

Geoffrey Woolley, a Second Lieutenant, was the first Territorial Army Officer to be awarded the VC. He was born in St Peter's Vicarage, Bethnal Green, in May 1892, and attended Parmiter's School. At 22, he was the sole officer commanding the survivors of Queen Victoria's Rifles against the Germans at Hill 60 in Belgium (1915) and held his post against orders until relieved. He followed his father into holy orders after the war collecting the Military Cross along the way. His image is on one of the 'VC Heroes' cigarette cards issued by Gallahers.

Scout Commissioner Roland Phillips was living and working in Stepney Green at the outbreak of the First World War – although he was an 'Honourable', the son of Viscount Lord St David. He joined the Army, at the age of twenty-four, receiving the Military Cross for conspicuous gallantry early in 1916, but was killed at the Somme just a few months later, when leading his men over the top. His death was described by Lord Baden-Powell as 'the heaviest our Brotherhood has sustained'. An insight into the man is revealed in the humour of one of his letters to Lady Baden-Powell (in 1915): 'Personally it will be the most wildly happy moment of my life, if when the war is over, I can go back with a Scout smile to continue to work amongst the boys of the East End . . . And it would not make an atom of difference that I happened to be deficit in eyes, or arms, or teeth, or any other of those handy little things that nearly everybody used to have before the war started.'

An unsung hero from the First World War was Arthur Lovell, a Limehouse costermonger, who was twice wounded and also remembered for lending a colleague a gas mask, saving his life. Arthur survived, only to die on the tenth anniversary of Armistice Day when he saved another life, that of a four-year-old girl, by pushing her out of the way of a truck, which killed him instead. He did merit the honour of a full military funeral, with the gun carriage followed by a costermonger's cart.

Dr Hannah Billig was born in Hanbury Street (Whitechapel) in 1901 and qualified as a doctor, setting up a surgery in Cable Street, hence references to her as 'The Angel of Cable Street'. She was awarded the George Medal (the civilian equivalent of the VC) for her efforts in helping the victims of the East End bombings during the Second World War, although sustaining injury herself. Not content with her wartime achievements, she joined the Indian Army Medical Corps and went to Bengal and Assam during the post-war famine, resulting in further recognition for her work in the form of an MBE which, incidentally, she was 'too busy' to collect from Buckingham Palace.

Bow engineer George Wyllie was part of the bomb disposal team working in London during the Second World War. When an unexploded bomb settled close by St Paul's Cathedral in September 1940, he and his team worked among burning gas mains for three days to prise it out of the earth. Having succeeded, they carried out a controlled explosion on Hackney Marshes, resulting in a 100ft crater. As a result, his was one of the first three George Crosses to be awarded.

8

DEATH & RELIGION

STRIKING CONVERSIONS

John Newton, born in Wapping in 1725, made three voyages as master of slave trading ships between 1750 and 1754, in spite of his (hypocritical?) religious convictions, landing his cargoes for sale near the Town of Ramsgate pub, Wapping. He is said to have had deep regrets about the barbaric trade later in life. In fact, he turned to hymn-writing (including 'Amazing Grace') and became the rector of St Mary Woolnoth in the City in his last years.

In 1886, Frederick Charrington (a celibate and temperate member of the Charrington Brewing dynasty) opened the Great Assembly Hall in Mile End Road as the largest prayer hall in Europe with 5,000 people attending every Sunday. He then set up a campaign against sexual immorality and was responsible for the closure of some 200 back-street brothels.

CEMETERIES WITH A DIFFERENCE

The first established cemetery in London for victims of the fourteenth-century Black Death was in the vicinity of East Smithfield. It covered around 2 hectares and is now known as the Royal Mint cemetery because of excavations on the site of the old Royal Mint (which had moved to Wales by 1980). Some 759 burials were excavated a few

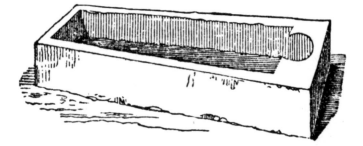

years after the Royal Mint moved out, the only large-scale excavation of its kind in the country, but a large part of the cemetery is believed to remain below the historic building.

The first Jewish community established in modern Britain (i.e. after Oliver Cromwell 'allowed' Jews back in to England for the first time in 300 years) was in Mile End Road in 1656. Once the hospital and retirement home for local Spanish and Portuguese Jews, Albert Stern House is now residential accommodation for Queen Mary College. The oldest Jewish burial ground (from 1657) remains here, concealed at the back of the building. The cemetery's burials include Benjamin Disraeli's grandfather in 1816 – but its location was probably not a welcome reminder of their destiny for the original residents of the nearby retirement home.

Victoria Park had its own 9-acre cemetery in its earlier years. Hundreds of funerals took place here every week, the favourite day being Sunday, most of them for children. The plot became Meath Gardens in 1895, designed by Fanny Wilkinson.

OUTSTANDING CHURCHES PAST AND PRESENT

The oldest building in Docklands is St Matthias Old Church in Poplar High Street, now a community centre. It is the only church in London that remains from the period when Cromwell was 'in charge' and has columns said to be formed from an Armada wreck.

The oldest surviving German church in England (from 1762) is St George's Lutheran Church in Alie Street, Aldgate. It was built by a wealthy German sugar-baker in the heart of a sugar refining district, and was restored in 2004. One of the most famous names in the baptismal records is Paul Reuter, born in Germany in 1816 but probably living in the area by 1845 when he was baptised (originally Israel Bere Josafat). The international news agency, Reuters, itself has a local connection, moving from Fleet Street (and other locations) to Canary Wharf in 2005.

When St George-in-the-East (in Cannon Street Road, Wapping) was bombed in 1941, a prefab was erected within its shell, and became the parish's home for seventeen years from December 1943: known as St Georges-in-the-Ruins.

The seventeenth-century St Paul's Church, Shadwell, was once known as the Church of Sea Captains when local residents such as Captain James Cook worshipped there – Cook's son was baptised there, too. More than seventy sea captains are buried in its grounds, although it has other claims to fame: John Wesley gave his last sermon here, Thomas Jefferson's mother (a local girl) was a regular until her move to America in 1735 when she was fifteen, and John Betjeman wrote about it.

St Dunstan's in Stepney dates from the fifteenth century, though an earlier wooden church was here from the tenth century. Over the main entrance is a pair of tongs – associated with St Dunstan (the patron saint of metal-workers) who was reputed to have tweaked the devil's nose with a hot pair. Another story is of the devil asking Dunstan to shoe a horse, which Dunstan attached to the devil's hoof only after obtaining a promise that the devil would never enter a house with a horseshoe outside (hence lucky horseshoes). In the eighteenth century, St Dunstan's became known as the church of the high seas – traditionally, any English child born at sea is regarded as a Stepney parishioner (i.e. 'born in Stepney') because most London-registered ships sailed from local docks. At one time, all births, deaths and marriages at sea were registered at St Dunstan's.

MORE CHURCH CHIT-CHAT

The largest church organ to survive in Britain from the eighteenth century is at the Grade I listed Christ Church, Spitalfields. All of its 2,126 pipes are currently being restored. The church is one of three Nicholas Hawksmoor churches in the East End, the others being St George-in-the-East, and St Anne's, Limehouse.

St Anne's, Commercial Road, Limehouse, also has an organ story; its pipe organ won first prize in the Great Exhibition of 1851. It is renowned as having (a) the highest public clock in the country – apart from Big Ben – on a 225ft steeple, visible, originally, by shipping on the Thames, and (b) a pyramid in its graveyard which had been intended, rather oddly, for its roof.

The last organ story, promise: St Botolph, Aldgate, has the oldest in London, dating back to 1676.

London's only floating church is St Peter's Barge, moored opposite the Docklands Museum in West India Dock since 2003. This particular church is a twenty-first century innovation, but would have been very useful in the days of sail.

The church of St Leonard in Shoreditch High Street dates back to at least the thirteenth century (though the present building dates from about 1735) and became known during Shakespeare's day as the actors' church, being near the original London theatres located here. Several of the Burbage lineage are buried here (famous actors of that period), as is Shakespeare's young nephew, and, later, Henry VIII's famous jester, Will Somers. It is believed to be the first church to be lit with gas mantles, probably due to its proximity to the Gas Light and Coke Company (of about 1817) – and is still frequented by local actors. St Leonard, interestingly, is the patron saint of prisoners, captives and slaves.

Twenty-six new churches were built in Stepney between 1823 and 1891, and twenty-eight churches closed in the same area between 1969 and 1990 including most of these 'newer' churches.

A FEW SURPRISES

The official home of Bow Bells is not Bow Church (or, more correctly, St Mary's Church in Bow) but St Mary-le-Bow in Cheapside. Cockneys 'born within the sound of Bow bells' are born within the sound of the City church, not the Bow church!

Of the 150 synagogues built for Jewish immigrants in the nineteenth century, only four now remain in the area. Similarly, of the eight French Protestant churches which arrived in the Spitalfields area between 1687 and 1743 (courtesy of the immigrant Huguenots) one survives on the corner of Fournier Street and Brick Lane: it has since been a Methodist chapel, a missionary hall, a synagogue, and is now a mosque. This building is the only building outside the Holy Land which has housed Christianity, Judaism and Islam.

In 1710, Mrs Elizabeth Goodlad was buried at St Dunstan's (often known as Stepney Church), at the grand old age of 99, not bad for the early eighteenth century – especially as she had given birth to twenty daughters, all buried here, too.

There is a written report (in Douglas Hay's *The Albion Tree*) of a gravedigger from St Dunstan, Thomas Jenkins, selling bodies to a private surgeon in London. He was caught, and sentenced to a public whipping. Tied to a cart, slowly pulled by cart horses, he was followed by a mob who encouraged the punishment, urging that he was not spared.

Towards the end of the eighteenth century, Sundays in the East End divided people between church-going and such pastimes as bull-baiting or dog-fighting, the religious option often losing out. The latter were held, among other places, in the churchyard of St Matthew's in Hereford Street, Bethnal Green. A bit too close, it seems, given that one terrified bull attempted to escape by running into the church during a Sunday morning service.

The first Swedish congregation in London rented a Baptist chapel in Ratcliff Highway in 1710, with their own church following eighteen years later in Prince's Square, Wapping, now Swedenborg Gardens. This was the Ulrika Eleonora church, which has since relocated. Jenny Lind, the 'Swedish Nightingale', is said to have attended services here. The first Danish church in London was also in this location (Prince's Square), and seems to pre-date the Swedish church by a dozen years but closed sometime between 1840 and 1850.

In 1870, Pope Pius IX was after a seamless silk garment to add to his extensive wardrobe. However, such a garment could only be hand-made and Spitalfields was the only place where a weaver could be found – a long way to go for a new outfit.

SOME UNUSUAL 'AFTER DEATH' EXPERIENCES

The pugilist and publican, Thomas Topham of Shoreditch, ended up killing his wife after a jealous row, and then killing himself. A sad end for the 'British Samson' who once twisted a kitchen spit round the neck of an ostler who had insulted him – and was able to lift three hogsheads of water (1,836lb). More unusually, however, it seems he achieved 'resurrection' a week later – or, as it was 1749, was he dug up by those acting for local surgeons perhaps?

After the theologian and visionary Emanuel Swedenborg died in 1772, he was buried in the Swedish church in what is now Swedenborg Gardens (then Prince's Square), Wapping. Much later, his remains were returned to his homeland (just before the First World War) and that should have been the end of it, but the remains had been missing the skull – which turned up nearly seventy years later in an auction at Sotheby's. The skull was bought by a Swedish professor for £1,500 and sent to join the rest of Swedenborg's body.

Richard Parker was hanged from the yard-arm of HMS *Sandwich* following his role as leader of the Nore mutiny in 1797, cheating the hangman by jumping overboard (complete with noose, thereby breaking his neck) rather than facing hanging until death. Initially swiftly buried in unconsecrated ground near Sheerness, Kent, his wife exhumed his body and smuggled it in a dung cart to Whitechapel, where he was finally laid to rest in the burial vault of St Mary Matfelon (long gone). Not something many wives have probably attempted.

A Chinese seaman, known as and buried as John Anthony, was the first Chinese person to be naturalised in the UK. It seems he amassed quite a fortune for looking after Chinese sailors as an agent for the East India Co. He was buried at Shadwell in August 1805, the place of his baptism, and the Chinese mourners were dressed in white, carrying lighted tapers, an intriguing sight.

John Williams, the main (but by no means proven) suspect in the Ratcliff Highway murders in 1811, was buried with a stake through his heart at the junction of Commercial Road and Cannon Street Road after committing suicide in prison. In 1886, his skeleton – complete with stake it seems – was discovered when the area was being excavated by a gas supplier, and claimed by the Crown and Dolphin public house nearby as a souvenir to display on their counter (the pub now a private house).

The *Graphic* (10 October 1874) reported an unusual walking funeral in Bethnal Green. The coffin had bird cages with black crêpe ties perched on top, complete with singing canaries. It seems the deceased, a bird-fancier, had wanted his 'pets' to accompany him beyond the grave – but whether this actually happened is not reported. In the same issue, there is reference to the funeral of a 'dog fancier' in Spitalfields, with every mourner accompanied by a dog; and that of a dahlia-grower followed by weavers carrying bouquets of these flowers. It seems dahlia shows were popular with weavers in Spitalfields.

In February 2008 when the undertakers from Co-op Funerals left their hearse and limousine in a car park in Poplar as they called in at the nearby chapel to check the flowers, they were unceremoniously clamped. Although released in time for the funeral as 'a goodwill gesture', it seems that even the dead are not safe from the rules that apply to the living.

A Dozen East End Ghost Stories

A black coach pulled by four black horses, with the hated Bishop Bonner inside, is said to have been spotted around the Victoria Park area. He died in 1569, the last and most hated (for his persecution of Protestants) of the bishops to own the Manor of Stepney.

The ghost of brewer Sir Benjamin Truman is said to haunt 91 Brick Lane where he lived in his grand Georgian house in the eighteenth century. Once the ghost was established, as such, a jug of stout was left in the drawing room every night for 'him' and was empty every morning. Sceptics will have a different explanation.

The Ragged School Museum in Copperfield Road, Mile End, had thousands of children through its doors when it was a school for the poor and destitute in the nineteenth (and early twentieth) century. It seems that some of these children, and teachers, never left because there have been regular reports ever since of children's voices, laughter, and of inexplicable temperature changes.

The Black Swan public house in Bow Road was bombed during September 1916 by a German Zeppelin, one of the earliest buildings to be destroyed in this way. The explosion killed two of the landlord's children (daughters Cissie and Sylvia), his baby granddaughter and their grandmother. The ghosts of Cissie and Sylvia were said to haunt the pub, even after it was rebuilt in 1920 (it was demolished in the 1970s).

The Hanging Judge, George Jeffreys, is said to haunt several locations (and why not?) including Wapping Old Stairs beside the Town of Ramsgate, the pub where he was captured in 1689.

Admiral Nelson, no less, is said to be waiting – still – for Lady Hamilton to join him at the Gun public house in Docklands. It seems they regularly – and secretly – met in what is now known as the River Room, bearing in mind that Nelson had a property nearby and visited the area regularly to inspect the naval guns being produced in the local foundries. His inspections of Lady Hamilton were less public.

Some of the Ripper victims are said to haunt the streets of Whitechapel – Mary Ann Nichol is reputedly the 'ghost in the gutter' around Durward Street, and Annie Chapman 'haunts' Hanbury Street.

Tapping noises, moans, heavy footsteps overhead, overturned chairs . . . classic signs of ghostly activity occurred in a house in Teesdale

Street, Bethnal Green, in 1938. Not just the local but the national press became excited by the reports from George Davis and his family, and at one point some 2,000 ghost hunters were photographed outside. As a result, the police had to cordon off the road. However, psychic investigators failed to find any real 'evidence' (in spite of the production of, amazingly, ghostly fingerprints!) and put the hauntings down to over-active imaginations.

Screams of pain and terror are said to be heard in the evenings at Bethnal Green tube station. This was the site of a 1943 disaster resulting from a panic-stricken crowd (a panic prompted by a non-existent air raid) when 173 were crushed to death and 92 seriously injured inside the entrance.

In 1972 a motorcyclist gave a lift to a boy from the south to the north end of Blackwall Tunnel – only to find on arrival that his passenger had vanished. He investigated the boy's address, their destination, to find the boy had died a number of years earlier.

The landlady of the Drivers' Arms in Lawton Road, Bow, called in a medium in 1979 after heavy objects started to move of their own accord, and drinks started disappearing. The medium blamed a Victorian tenant who disapproved of women drinking!

In an office building near Stepney Green station a ghost was reported in the 1980s – or rather the smell of one. The offices were built on the site of a former doctor's surgery, and staff could smell embalming fluid – strong, sweet and sickly. What had that doctor been up to?

RELIGIOUS CONNECTIONS

John Wesley's mother, Susannah, was born in Spital Yard in 1669. John was one of nineteen children and, when establishing his numerous Methodist societies, is said to have preached at Spitalfields, St Paul's in Shadwell, St John's in Wapping and St Matthew's in Bethnal Green.

Thomas Cromwell, who lived at Great Place, Stepney, near St Dunstan's, was the man who established the supremacy of the monarch over the church so that Henry VIII could marry Anne Boleyn.

The bells of Aldgate, Shoreditch and Stepney are all mentioned in the nursery rhyme 'Oranges and Lemons'. But the 'great bell of Bow' is a reference to St Mary-le-Bow Church in the City of London (Cheapside).

The Jews' Free School, established in 1817 in Bell Lane, Spitalfields, for the rapidly increasing Jewish population in the area, became the largest school in the British Empire by the end of the nineteenth century with 3,000 students. It moved to Camden Town in 1958.

The informal Petticoat Lane 'Parliament' pre-Second World War, made up of Jewish men with extremely strong opinions, had an unusual meeting place – the large underground gents' toilets in nearby Leyden Street.

On Good Fridays in the nineteenth century, it was a tradition for sailors in the East End docks to make a figure of Judas from wood and straw that they then flogged (literally) to pieces before throwing it overboard.

William Booth's Salvation Army (previously the East London Christian Mission) was formed at a meeting in Whitechapel Road in 1878. Booth had been cultivating interest in his work by preaching the gospel in the area, for example outside the Blind Beggar,

Whitechapel Road, and even in a tent in Bakers Row (1865) until a strong gust of wind blew it down. By the time he died in 1912, the Salvation Army was established in fifty-eight countries (and has continued to spread).

When Miriam Moses became Mayor of Stepney in 1931, she made history as the first Jewish woman in England to achieve that office. Her involvement (both before and after 1931) in many local community organisations resulted in an OBE and an appearance on *This is Your Life*.

Tower Hamlets has the largest Muslim population in the UK, hence the six-storey East London Mosque and London Muslim Centre in Whitechapel Road, which can house 5,000 worshippers. It also has one of the largest Buddhist centres – the London Buddhist Centre at the junction of Roman Road and Globe Road, utilising a former fire station.

DEATHS WITH A DIFFERENCE

If the burial register of St Leonard's Church, Shoreditch, can be believed, when Thomas Cam died in 1588 he was 207!

The death of Sarah Whittock, a widow from Wellington Street, Stepney, aged sixty, was reported in the *Penny Illustrated* of 21 July 1866. She had been visiting a cousin, kissing her goodbye on the steps outside her front door – but both ladies ended up at the bottom of the steps in a heap, and poor Mrs Whittock died in hospital.

When orphaned Bow teenager Alice Coborn became engaged, she planned her wedding for her fifteenth birthday (not particularly young for a bride in the seventeenth century). Instead, young Alice died of smallpox – and was buried on her wedding day. Her grieving fiancé carved a statue of young Alice and placed it in St Mary's Church (Bow Road) as part of her memorial.

In 1910, people were so desperate to get into an election meeting (!) in Stepney Town Hall, Cable Street, that they pushed over the iron railings outside. The railings collapsed, taking some of the crowd and two massive stone pillars with them. Those injured (and the one man unfortunately killed) did not get to hear what William Wedgwood Benn, the MP for St George's-in-the-East (and father of Tony Benn), had to say.

When a sightseer visited Millwall docks during the building of the *Great Eastern* (1853–8), he stood gazing up in awe rather closer than he should – and was struck dead by a monkey wrench dropped from far above.* The jinxed *Great Eastern* not only resulted in the loss of lives of spectators on the slipway which collapsed at her launch, and the loss of lives of some of her workmen (including a riveter's mate impaled on a scaffolding support), but the explosion once she did make it out of the Thames Estuary killed six stokers. The skeleton of yet another worker, possibly a riveter who had gone missing, was found in a sealed space between the inner and outer hulls when the unlucky ship was finally dismantled in 1888.

MORE THAN ITS FAIR SHARE OF TRAGEDIES

During the Great Plague of 1665, some 600 corpses a week were disposed of in Stepney alone during the summer months.

In February 1882, two trains collided between Old Ford station and the Fairfield Road bridge. The wood from the broken railway carriages was made into bonfires so that porters and labourers from the station could see what they were doing in trying to assist the injured, over a dozen of whom were taken in convoy to the London Hospital. Five people died as a result of the collision, all East Enders.

The nineteenth-century cholera outbreak in Poplar, Stepney and Whitechapel was detailed in the *Penny Illustrated* (11 August 1866), with the area described as including 'almost every nationality on the earth from the Fin to the Laskar, from the Chinese opium smoker to the rum-drinking negro sailor.' This was before such publications had come across stereotypes.

---

* A conflicting story has his head jammed in a press, but I'm with the monkey wrench.

EXEMPLARY VICARS

John Colet, who became Dean of St Paul's in 1504, was St Dunstan's most famous vicar, with a house at White Horse Street, Ratcliff. The grander Great Place in Stepney Green became the rural retirement home for his mother – well deserved when it is revealed that she had had twenty-two children, only John surviving into adulthood. He was a contemporary of Erasmus and Thomas More, both personal friends. William Jerome, vicar of St Dunstan's, was burned alive in 1540 for preaching an Anabaptist sermon, during which he referred to MPs as 'butterflies, fools and knaves'. Some things never change.

The Revd Mr Bartlett of St Saviour's Church, Poplar, regularly went hop-picking with his parishioners in the mid-twentieth century.

George Carey, Archbishop of Canterbury from 1991 to 2002, was born in Bow, the son of a hospital porter. He was the first in this position not to have attended Oxford or Cambridge.

John Sentamu, formerly Bishop of Stepney, became the Church of England's first black Archbishop (of York) in 2005. He had fled Uganda, where he was a judge, after being persecuted by Idi Amin.

9

COCKNEY CULTURE

SHAKESPEARE AND HIS CRONIES IN THE EAST

Early theatrical performances were staged in inn-yards such as the Boar's Head, Whitechapel, the George or the Red Lion in Stepney (mid-sixteenth century). In September 1557, the Lord Mayor of London stopped a 'lewde playe' being performed at the Boar's Head, probably the earliest 'theatre' in the East End. These venues were soon followed by the first playhouse in England: the Theatre, built by Shakespearean performer James Burbage in Shoreditch in 1577 at the back of the George. Shakespeare was one of the original players, although seemingly he also was employed at one point to hold the patrons' horses . . . more reliably, it is claimed that *Romeo and Juliet* (and others) debuted here. After a dispute over the lease, the 600ft-diameter theatre was dismantled in 1599 and rebuilt south of the River Thames, becoming the Globe. The Curtain Theatre (named after the striped curtain outside) had by then set up in competition close to the Theatre's original site.

HORSE
SHAKESPEARE
& I.

MORE LITERARY CONNECTIONS

The Grapes in Narrow Street, Limehouse, was the apparent inspiration for the Six Jolly Fellowship Porters in *Our Mutual Friend* with its 'corpulent windows' and riverside setting. *Nicholas Nickleby* features the time the hero spent at a 'little cottage at Bow' in the country. In *Pickwick Papers*, there is a description of the Bull Inn at Aldgate, a place where stagecoaches started out on the road to Ipswich. *Oliver Twist* features Bill Sykes's den in Bethnal Green 'in a maze of the mean and dirty streets' and Fagin is reputedly based on a Jewish 'fence' from Spitalfields called Isaac 'Ikey' Solomon. Mile End is referred to as a poor and 'thronged' area in *The Uncommercial Traveller*, and Ratcliff Highway is described as a 'reservoir of dirt, drunkenness and drabs' in *Sketches By Boz*. Note: Charles Dickens, who wrote all these of course, often visited his godfather, Christopher Huffam, who ran his sail-making business from Newell Street, Limehouse.

Colonel Jack, by Daniel Defoe, is about a character brought up in Goodman's Fields, with references to areas around the Rag Fair then at Rosemary Lane. Similarly, Moll Flanders visits Whitechapel, Petticoat Lane, and Bow on her travels.

Bram Stoker's Dracula is said to have stored six boxes of earth (for his night time repose) at 197 Chicksand Street, Mile End Old Town.

Gulliver (of *Gulliver's Travels*) lived in Wapping before going off on the adventures penned by Jonathan Swift.

The People of the Abyss was written by Jack London after a fact-finding mission to Flower and Dean Street in 1902, a destination that baffled local taxi drivers who had seemingly never taken anyone there before, because of its slum location. He is also said to have visited Poplar workhouse while in the area.

Limehouse Nights, 1916, achieved immortality when it was banned for immorality by the National Subscription Library. It was written by Thomas Burke, a one-time Poplar resident.

There are scenes in George Orwell's *Down and Out in Paris and London* set in a Limehouse lodging house (which he visited for research), an area he describes as 'sprinkled with Orientals . . . even a few Sikhs'. In *Nineteen Eighty-Four*, Orwell refers to bombs falling on a crowded theatre in Stepney.

The Picture of Dorian Gray by Oscar Wilde features Dorian visiting an opium den in Limehouse.

The old Limehouse China Town area (Gill Street, etc.) was the setting for the *Legend of Fu Manchu* and another dozen Fu Manchu thrillers, with a heavy emphasis on opium dens, although author Sax Rohmer (born Arthur Ward) never visited the area.

To Sir With Love was inspired by the experiences of E.R. Braithwaite, a Guyanese teacher in the East End after the Second World War. He taught at St George's-in-the East School, Stepney, and Bigland Street School. It was also made into a film starring Sidney Poitier.

Ruby in the Smoke by Philip Pullman is set in the unsavoury rat-ridden alleys of nineteenth-century Wapping. The book became a BBC1 drama.

The fictional Richard Sharpe (*Sharpe's Tiger*, etc. etc. etc. by Bernard Cornwell) was brought up in a 'foundling home' in Brewhouse Lane, Wapping, before moving 'up North', providing Sean Bean with the excuse for his accent in the filmed versions.

Dan Leno and the Limehouse Golem by Peter Ackroyd is a Victorian murder mystery.

NOT FORGETTING POETRY

Even non-East Enders have taken an interest in the area. T.S. Eliot's 'The Waste Land' incorporates a reference to:

> Drifting logs
> Down Greenwich reach
> To the Isle of Dogs

Or, for a more Cockney take, 'What's O'clock in Poplar' from C.C. Martindale:

> Through the twisted twigs a breeze
> Whispers restlessly – 'Oh yes!
> Even in Poplar we have trees –
> Vine and fig-tree, Miss, no less!'

A LIST OF LITERARY SURPRISES

Geoffrey Chaucer wrote in the *Canterbury Tales* of the Priory of St Leonard's (in Bromley-by-Bow) as a place with a 'nonne, a prioresse, that of hir smylying was ful sympl and coy'. Chaucer's father owned a number of shops in Whitechapel (in the fourteenth century) and Chaucer himself stayed in rooms near Aldgate between 1374 and 1386.

Queen Elizabeth I's advisors took exception to a satirical comedy called the *Isle of Dogs* and threw one of its authors (Ben Jonson) and two actors into prison. Described as lewd and scandalous, it has not survived . . . (who said 'shame'?)

Shakespeare has a few passing mentions of the East End: Mile End Green in *Henry IV, Part 2* (Act 3), where Justice Shallow was a student; and the Porter's term 'limbs of Limehouse' in *Henry VIII* (Act 5, Scene 3), a probable reference to local mariners. The man himself was thought to have lived in the vicinity when the Theatre in Shoreditch was up and running, although there is no real evidence of that.

Diarist Samuel Pepys' mother Margaret was born in Whitechapel as Margaret Kite, from the family of a local butcher. His friend Sir William Ryder (or Rider) lived off Roman Road and, during the Great Fire of London, Pepys stored his valuables – including his diary – there for safety.

Daniel Defoe was married (to Mary) at St Botolph's in Aldgate in January 1684, more than thirty years before *Robinson Crusoe* appeared. He was, at the time, a hosier in the wholesale trade.

It was the widow of Revd Ralph Cawley of St Dunstan's, Stepney, who taught Jane and Cassandra Austen (at Oxford) in the 1780s.

American writer, Phillis Wheatley (*Phillis* was the name of the slave ship that took her from Africa to the Wheatley family) could not find a publisher for her poetry in America at a time of segregation, so Archibald Bell, from 'No. 8 Aldgate Street, near The Saracen's Head' came to her rescue in 1773. He published her *Poems on Various Subjects, Religious and Moral*, believed to be the first book by a black woman in the English-speaking world.

The author of *Three Men in a Boat* – Jerome K. Jerome – lived as a boy for seven years at 47 Sussex Street, Poplar, after his family moved to London in the 1860s.

When Oscar Wilde was released from prison on 19 May 1897, the man who was there to support him (the same man who had escorted him to and from his trial) was Stewart Headlam, the curate of St Matthew's in Bethnal Green.

Before becoming a successful writer, Joseph Conrad was a merchant seaman who often stayed at the Sailors' Home and Red Ensign Club, Dock Street, Whitechapel.

In 1971, Chris Searle was fired from his teaching job at Sir John Cass School (Stepney) after he published a book of poems written by his pupils which was regarded as too negative (*Stepney Words*). He had published the book without the permission of the governors and, when he was fired, 500 pupils went on strike. They were obliged to return to their lessons after a matter of days, but it took Mr Searle two years to get his job back.

LIBRARIES HAVE STORIES TOO

While local councils dragged their feet in establishing public libraries for the East End proletariat, two wealthy individuals stepped in: John Passmore Edwards and Andrew Carnegie (in the 1890s). Edwards paid for free libraries in Shoreditch, Whitechapel, Poplar and elsewhere (as well as helping to establish Whitechapel Art Gallery), and Carnegie financed the library at Cubitt Town, Isle of Dogs (one of 2,505 libraries he financed around the world). The Passmore Edwards Library building in Commercial Road, Limehouse, is now Grade II listed.

Limehouse Library had an interesting exhibit in its entrance until as recently as the Second World War – a display of species of fish that had been caught in the River Lea between 1876 and 1881, many of which had won prizes.

Bethnal Green Library, which opened in Bethnal Green Gardens in 1922, occupies the site of the largest of several mental asylums in the area, hence the gardens' local name of Barmy Park. Its most distinguished inmate had been scholarly Scot Alexander Cruden who 'lost his reason' after his fiancée had a child by her brother. He escaped by sawing through the bedstead to which he was chained (on his birthday, in 1738) but, although detained at Aldgate wearing just one slipper, he was allowed his freedom having already spent ten weeks in Bethnal House.

The Women's Library in Old Castle Street, Aldgate, houses the most extensive collection of women's history in the world. It is located behind the façade of the Whitechapel Baths which closed in 1990.

The Whitechapel Library – the first library in the East End – was also the first to stock Somali texts for its customers. It closed as a library in 2005, but the building was taken over by the expanding Whitechapel Art Gallery.

Around the East End, libraries as an institution are being replaced by Idea Stores, which incorporate traditional library services with the addition of classes, corporate facilities, community events, cultural activities and information centres. The Whitechapel 'store' surpassed the loan of a million books in one year between April 2009 and March 2010 for the first time.

Six Painters Who Lived In The East End

Sir Peter Paul Rubens stayed with one of his models, the wife of Sir Balthazar Gerbier, and her family in Bethnal Green between 1629 and 1630. (Possibly Netteswell House in Old Ford Road, later the home of the curator of Bethnal Green Museum.)

Maritime painter Francis Holman lived variously at Bell Dock (Wapping) and Old Gravel Lane (St George's-in-the-East) in the eighteenth century. One of his subjects was East Indiamen, a type of frigate, and another was the Thames-side shipbuilding yards.

Joseph Mallord William Turner inherited a pub in Wapping by the name of the Ship and Bladebone – but it is a pub called Turner's Old Star Pub which remains nearby (off Wapping Lane). He is said to have visited Wapping for inspiration, especially for 'The Fighting Temeraire' (1838) which could have been seen on the nearby river when it was being dragged to the breaker's yard. When in Wapping, he posed as Admiral Booth, the surname being that of the widow he lived with in a more salubrious part of London.

James McNeill Whistler rented rooms in Wapping from 1859 to about 1864. During this time he produced some renowned views of the area, and many etchings. You need to go a long way to see his painting called 'Wapping', however. It is on display at the National Gallery of Art, Washington DC, bearing in mind that Whistler was an American.

Francis Bacon lived in Narrow Street, Limehouse, for a while, when he was a regular at the Waterman's Arms on the Isle of Dogs.

Thomas Stothard, Royal Academician and illustrator of contemporary publications of *The Pilgrim's Progress* and *Robinson Crusoe*, lived with his mother in Stepney in the 1770s.

TWELVE PAINTINGS DEPICTING THE EAST END

'Launch of the *Venerable*, 74 Guns, at Blackwall': 1784, Francis Holman (National Maritime Museum).

'View of Mr Perry's Yard, Blackwall': 1796, William Dixon (National Maritime Museum).

'Wapping': 1807, Thomas Rowlandson – a scene in a sailor's tavern (National Maritime Museum).

'Limehouse Reach': *c.* 1820, William Anderson (National Maritime Museum).

'The Hay Market, Whitechapel, Looking East': *c.* 1835, anon (Guildhall Art Gallery, London).

'Wapping': 1861, James McNeill Whistler, (The National Gallery of Art, Washington DC).

'Blackwall Yard from The Thames': 1866, Francis Holman (National Maritime Museum).

'View of Northumberland Head Inn, corner Gun Street and Fort Street, Stepney': 1884, John Crowther (London Metropolitan Archives in Clerkenwell).

'View of Bow Churchyard': 1887, John Crowther (London Metropolitan Archives in Clerkenwell).

'Open Window, Spitalfields': 1981, Anthony Eyton (Tate Gallery).

'Portrait of Zarrin Kashi Overlooking Whitechapel High Street': 1981, Leonard McComb (Tate Gallery).

'Christchurch, Spitalfields, Morning': 1990, Leon Kossoff (Tate Gallery).

More Artistic Connections

The first gold medal winner of the Royal Academy of Arts in 1775 was John Bacon, a Spitalfields resident.

Gustave Doré was responsible for a large number of wood engravings depicting the East End of 1872 in a depressing light. The slum areas of Bluegate Fields, Shadwell, for instance, are not the most obvious choice of composition for a Victorian artist.

Whitechapel Art Gallery was founded in 1901 in Whitechapel High Street with over 200,000 visitors to its first show. It has since become famous for the British premieres of such artists as Pablo Picasso, Jackson Pollock, Mark Rothko and Frida Kahlo. Picasso's famous anti-war painting 'Guernica' was seen at the gallery in 1938 on its first visit to Britain, and returned, in tapestry form, in 2009. More recently, Gilbert and George and Mark Wallinger have featured. The building is Grade II listed.

The Chisenhale Gallery, Chisenhale Road, Bow, is in a converted veneer factory and offers solo exhibitions, mainly by the up and coming.

Henry Moore, the UK's most famous sculptor, was also a war artist (Second World War) and embarked upon a series of pencil drawings of East End underground shelters. One location was Cable Street, depicting the arches under the railway line.

Twenty-first-century Spitalfields has the highest density of artists in Europe, including Tracey Emin and Gilbert and George.

ARTY SURPRISES

When the Stifford Estate in Stepney was demolished in 1997, Henry Moore's 1957 sculpture of 'Draped Seated Woman' was loaned to the Yorkshire Sculpture Park to avoid being vandalised . . . and it's still there. Worth anything between £4,000,000 and £24,000,000, the insurance for this striking work of art is still apparently being paid by Tower Hamlets Council.

The 1993 Turner Prize, won by Rachel Whiteread, was in part a result of her concrete and plaster cast of the interior of the last house remaining in Grove Road, Bow – named, aptly, 'House'. Placed in situ, it was not so popular with residents, and was pulled down a year later.

Lasting rather longer, but just as controversial, is the tree of 'stoplights' – a kind of elaborate traffic light structure – on a roundabout at Marsh Wall on the Isle of Dogs. It was created by Pierre Vivant to imitate the adjacent plane trees and the never-ending rhythm of the area. Quite.

In 2005, artist Helena Roden erected two giant (over 5 metres tall) anemones in Lefevre Park, Bow, to show the contrast between the old and ugly and the new and beautiful.

TWENTY FILMS UTILISING EAST END SETTINGS

It Always Rains on Sunday, 1947 (Bethnal Green, especially the bomb sites).

A Kid for Two Farthings, 1955 (Petticoat Lane and Aldgate), written by East Ender Wolf Mankowitz.

Sparrows Can't Sing, 1962 (Whitechapel and Shadwell), with lots of East Enders in the cast, including Barbara Windsor.

Gandhi, 1982 (Kingsley Hall, Bow).

The Long Good Friday, 1980 (Wapping and West India Quay).

Nineteen Eighty Four, 1984 (Richard Burton's last film), included Cheshire Street, Bethnal Green, as a location.

Full Metal Jacket, 1987 (Isle of Dogs abandoned dockyard).

Chaplin, 1992 (Wilton's Music Hall – though exterior shots are in central London).

Interview with the Vampire, 1994, made use of Grace's Alley and Ensign Street.

Sliding Doors, 1998 (Trinity Buoy Wharf), featured Fat Boys Diner.

Lock, Stock and Two Smoking Barrels, 1998 (Bethnal Green), included shots inside the Repton Boys' club in Cheshire Street.

The World is Not Enough, 1999, utilised Billingsgate Market and river locations around Blackwall Basin for the boat chase.

Secrets and Lies, 1996, features Quilter Street, Bethnal Green.

Guy Ritchie's *Snatch*, 2000 (Bethnal Green), the pawn shop was in Teesdale Street.

The Shiner, 2001 (Bethnal Green and surrounds), York Hall used for the boxing scenes.

Love Actually, 2003, featured the escalator in Canary Wharf station.

Vera Drake, 2004, utilised Cressy House in Stepney Green.

The Bourne Supremacy, 2004 (Canary Wharf).

Batman Begins, 2005, features the restaurant Plateau in Canada Place on the Isle of Dogs.

Hereafter, 2010, was filmed in part in Spitalfields – Bell Lane and Café le Jardin.

TEN TELEVISION PROGRAMMES FILMED IN THE EAST END

Bad Girls, 1999–2006, had an episode featuring the Marriott Hotel, West India Quay.

Bleak House, 2005, BBC1 production, featuring the Jellyby household in Spitalfields.

The Bill (various episodes since 1984 utilising Docklands, Roman Road, etc.).

Ashes to Ashes (Tobacco Dock). Specifically: – Series 1, episode 6, 2008.

London's Burning, 1988–2002 (Wapping). Note: not Blackwall as mentioned . . . confusing, yes.

Goodnight Sweetheart, 1993–9 (Bethnal Green), Ezra Street is 'Ducketts Passage'.

Bugs, (Docklands) 1995–9, e.g. 'Manna from Heaven' episode (1995) features Limehouse Link.

Big Breakfast (the Lock Keeper's Cottage, Old Ford Lock) launched in 1992.

Waking the Dead episodes in 2001 filmed in Bethnal Green.

Little Britain since 2003 (Lou and Andy's flat located on Cranbrook Estate, Bethnal Green).

Also, Limehouse Studios, operating from Canary Wharf in the 1980s, produced *Spitting Image, Who Dares Wins* and *Whose Line Is It Anyway?*

MORE STORIES OF THE BIG SCREEN

The first few *Carry On* scripts were written by Norman Hudis, born in Stepney in 1923. His *Carry On Nurse* was the top grossing UK film for 1959. After moving to the USA in the 1960s, he started making real money with scripts for *Hawaii Five-O* and *The Man from U.N.C.L.E.* among others.

The 1960 film *The Siege of Sidney Street* was shot in Dublin, and not in Sidney Street, because Dublin looked more like the real thing! Similarly, the 1990 film *The Krays* was filmed (mostly) in Greenwich.

The musical director of Hammer Films, from 1963 until his death in 1993, was Whitechapel-born musician Philip Martell.

The first Asian cinema in the East End was the Naz in Brick Lane which opened in 1967. It lasted ten years, and is now the Naz Café.

Tyrone Walker-Hebborn, an interesting mix of entrepreneur and roofer, was undeterred by the holes in the roof of what is now the Genesis Cinema in Whitechapel Road (the former ABC, which had been derelict for ten years). As a result, he not only took on the building and its renaissance (in the 1990s) but has gone on to produce his own films. A double whammy.

One of London's largest media production studios is set in the historic Three Mills area (hence its name, er, Three Mills Studios) with sixteen film stages in 20 acres.

The Blue Lamp (1950) was based on the true story of the murder of a policeman in Leman Street, Aldgate.

And The Little Screen

Everyone knows about *East Enders*, but these were also hit series about the East End:

Till Death Do Us Part (set in Wapping 1965–75), Alf Garnett supposedly named after Garnet Street.

Never Mind the Quality, Feel the Width (sitcom set in Whitechapel 1967–71).

Casualty 1906 and *Casualty 1907* were twenty-first-century drama series based on true archive stories at the Royal London Hospital – although they were not filmed there.

The Importance Of Language

Cockney Rhyming Slang may be slowly disappearing, but the following terms are immersed in the English language:

I should cocoa = I should say so
'Taters = cold (from potatoes in the mould)
Use your loaf = use your head (loaf of bread)
Let's scapa (or scarper) = scapa flow (go)

She can rabbit = talk (rabbit and pork)
My Old Dutch = wife (Duchess of Fife)
My old china = mate (china plate)
Dog and bone = telephone
Whistle = suit (whistle and flute)
Ruby = curry (Ruby Murray)
Boracic = skint (boracic lint)

NOT FORGETTING THE CLASSICAL WORLD

Although he was the first to play the organ at Christ Church, Spitalfields, Peter Prelleur from Rose Lane (an eighteenth-century Huguenot who became famous for his compositions, including his hymns) was not averse to spending his evenings playing harpsichord in the Angel and Crown, Whitechapel.

Musical prodigy, Solomon Cutner from Fournier Street (Spitalfields) played his first Tchaikovsky overture at the age of 6 in 1908 and made his debut at the Proms under Sir Henry Wood in 1914. Cutner became one of the most in-demand concert pianists not just in the UK but in the USA. He died in 1988.

The Art Deco, Grade II listed Troxy in Commercial Road reopened in 1963 after a three-year closure – as the London Opera Centre. It was run by the Royal Opera House at Covent Garden, and used mainly for rehearsals, scenery construction and storage. The location was also used for operatic training until 1977, with students including tenor Edmund Barham.

SOME COCKNEY SURPRISES

Pearly Kings and Queens may be associated with the East End, but they originated with Henry Croft, raised in Somers Town, the King's Cross area of North London.

Steptoe and Son were not Cockneys – the series was set in West London.

East Enders is not filmed in the East End.

10

NATURAL HISTORY

VICKY PARK

Victoria Park (The People's Park) remains the oldest public park in Britain, its construction starting in 1842, and being open to the public from 1845. In its early days, it offered everything an East Ender could desire: tennis courts, a bowling green, cricket nets, an athletic track, an aviary and a deer enclosure. Some 700 fruit trees growing on the original 88 hectares (now some 86) were replaced in 1845 by evergreens, because it was thought that fruit trees caused 'disorder' but the canals on the west and south boundaries were retained.

The East End equivalent of Speakers' Corner (in Hyde Park) was located alongside the elaborate drinking fountain until after the First World War. During the Second World War performances were staged by the touring Sadler's Wells Ballet company.

A lido – replacing the original bathing pond – was opened in 1936 accommodating up to 1,000 bathers but this was demolished in 1990. The original bathing pond is now used by anglers. Until as recently as 1985, twice-weekly modern and old-time dances were held.

During the Second World War, when the park was closed, it served as an anti-aircraft site, and a PoW camp for Germans and Italians. Years later, it was one of the venues for 'political' rock concerts against the Anti-Nazi League.

MORE OPEN SPACES

Annual fairs (usually in springtime) were a feature of the East End in the nineteenth century. The Stepney and Bow Fairs were popular on a grand scale, with as many as 200,000 attending the Easter Monday Fair at Stepney in 1844. Both were gone by 1860. The Rag Fair in Rosemary Lane around the same time was rather different – the entrance fee was 'von halfpenny' and all that was for sale was, yep, rags.

Before Victoria Park was formed, there were smaller 'pleasure gardens' in the East End, e.g. the New Globe Pleasure Gardens at Mile End, featuring fireworks and concerts, and the Jews Spring Gardens in Stepney.

When Tower Hamlets Cemetery closed in 1966, having been bombed five times during the Second World War, its 29-plus acres were set to become the largest woodland area in East London. The area was declared a Local Nature Reserve and a Conservation Area in 2000. Now the public can enjoy the park, the chalk maze and the Scrapyard Meadow. There is even a touch of the Sahara in the Soanes Centre which provides an arid ecosystem.

Mile End Park (36 hectares) is a much later venture, dating from the latter part of the twentieth century, utilising a Second World War bomb-site. Both the park and its Green Bridge (spanning the A11, a busy trunk road, to link the two halves of the park) have won a number of awards and incorporate such features as a terraced garden, a sports stadium and an ecology park that includes a wind turbine and climbing wall. It even features a number of wooden posts each illustrating Pythagoras' theorem, labelled 'Maths Year 2000'. From the cerebral to the practical, it also features the first silent electric go-karts in London, and in 2009 some parts became the first outdoor public places in Britain to be made smoke-free. Joanna Lumley is said to be a fan and has recorded Britain's first 'audio map' for blind visitors to the park.

St George's Gardens are located on The Highway with entrances from Cable Street. The former churchyard grounds surround the Nicholas Hawksmoor-designed Church of St George's-in-the-East.

For a different kind of open space, Shadwell Basin incorporates 7 acres with access directly to the Thames. Beginners and experts are catered for by the range of activities offered – windsurfing, canoeing, orienteering, sub-aqua, dragon boating, kayaking, sailing, power-boating and more.

Mudchute Park and Farm on the Isle of Dogs (Pier Street) was created from spoil and silt from the construction of Millwall Docks. The park (which housed gun emplacements during the Second World War) makes up more than half of the open spaces on the 'island' and incorporates wooded glades, a nature trail, allotments and a riding school. The farm houses goats, sheep, pigs, horses, cows, ducks and geese, many of which are suitable for petting, and is the biggest urban farm in Europe.

Farm animals can also be seen at Stepping Stones Farm in Stepney Way, which could be hiding the remains of a historic palace under a cow field. A smaller farm also in E1 (about 1 acre compared to 4) is Spitalfields City Farm in Buxton Street, off Brick Lane, built on the site of a former railway goods yard. This boasts characters such as Itchy the Kune-Kune sow from New Zealand, and Bayleaf the donkey.

King Edward Memorial Park was formerly Shadwell fish market and at one time the only public space between the Tower of London and the Isle of Dogs. The circular brick edifice was the ventilation shaft for Marc Brunel's record-breaking tunnel under the Thames.

Weavers' Fields (named after the silk weavers which once dominated the area) near Brick Lane offers twenty-first-century festivals – the annual Baishakhi Mela Festival, for instance, celebrating the Bengali new year, brings in as many as 100,000 visitors (Boris Johnson, the London Mayor, made it his first public engagement in 2008). It confirms its modern approach not just with the modern sculptures that abound, but with regard to its sustainability, rejecting the use of peat, herbicides and even excessive water.

In Tower Hamlets alone, there are over 160 parks, gardens and squares! The newest is Jubilee Park, built above Canary Wharf railway station on the Isle of Dogs with over 200 Metasequoia trees.

GARDENS MERITING A MENTION

Back in the fourteenth century, Henry Daniel grew over 250 different kinds of plants in his large Stepney garden before becoming a Dominican friar. Having spent seven years training as a physician and renowned as a herbalist, many of the plants reflected his interests.

The gardens of Kirby Castle (sixteenth century) produced tobacco as well as fruit and flowers. The owner (Hugh Platt) even made wine from locally grown grapes – and it was he who discovered how to preserve bottled fruit by excluding air. Sir Francis Drake was among his customers.

One of the earliest nursery gardens in London (dating from the 1640s) belonged to Leonard Gurle. He owned 12 acres between Brick Lane and Greatorex Street, and, by the 1670s, this nursery was the largest in London. It seems his fame grew as a result of the fruit trees he was renowned for (e.g. dwarf plums and French pears), but he also sold cypresses, honeysuckle, shrubs and seeds to the aristocracy and gentry. He also came up with a new nectarine which he named Elruge – his name spelt backwards with an additional E. In 1677, Gurle became the King's Gardener, having by then a second nursery in London Fields.

Malplaquet House, just off Mile End Road, is a large merchant's house built in 1741, now privately owned. It is not just the building, however, but the small outside area that is such an oasis in this part of London. The courtyard garden boasts a rare fernery, and uses local paving and Tudor Bricks in its planning, with plenty of quirky sculptures, and bark mulch to encourage the ferns, roses, fig trees and clematis. It is not often open to the public, understandably, as it is very much lived in.

John Wesley wrote of James Gordon's 'curious garden at Mile End' in 1775. It seems to have been James Gordon who introduced the China Rose, and who was instrumental in the survival of the camellia, introduced to Britain in 1739. His garden was described by at least one contemporary botanist as 'beautiful and . . . abundant'. Employed as head gardener to Lord Petre (based in Essex), he added to his income by selling seeds at Fenchurch Street, over the City border.

Scrap Iron Park was the nineteenth-century nickname for what is now Island Gardens on the Isle of Dogs. The original development –

incorporating villas and a plantation – failed: no villas were built and the plantation was neglected. By the 1880s, it had become a derelict dumping ground but was opened as a public park in 1895, notable for its spectacular views across to Greenwich as depicted by Canaletto.

Cable Street Community Gardens, between Shadwell and Limehouse DLR stations, is dedicated to growing organic flowers and vegetables without pesticides. It was founded on derelict land in the 1970s as part of a Friends of the Earth initiative.

LOOK OUT FOR THESE IN THE VICINITY

Dog rose (its hips rich in vitamin C)
Passion flower (not passion fruit)
Fat hen (can be eaten – like spinach)
Red clover (revered by the Romans)
Wild cherry (especially in parks)
Crab apple (sour apples, good for jelly)
Juniper (medicinal, as per the sixteenth-century Spitalfields apothecary, Nicholas Culpeper)
Lemon balm (relative of the mint family)
Chamomile (becoming scarce)
Elderflower (causes rather colourful bird droppings)
Mountain ash (small edible berries)
Sycamore (woodland areas, e.g. St Jude's Nature Park, Bethnal Green)
Silver birch (one of seventeen varieties of tree in Victoria Park)
London rocket (a priority species in the Tower Hamlets Biodiversity Action Plan)
Rosebay Willowherb (one of the first wild flowers to grow on bomb sites)
Carob trees (known as St John's bread) outside the Royal London Hospital, Mile End Road.

Ten Sites Of Importance For Nature Conservation (SINCS)

Spitalfields Viaduct (colourful range of wild flowers dominated by the butterfly bush)
Wapping Park, with impressive plane trees
Swedenborg Gardens (new woodland area)
Disused railway at Bow, notable for its sycamore trees (near Bow Church station)
St Jude's Nature Park
St George-in-the-East Church gardens
Weavers' Fields
Ion Square Gardens, Bethnal Green (incorporates small wildlife area)
Shadwell Basin, part of the Old London Docks
Perring Community Garden (organic garden and allotments for residents on site of an old air raid shelter)

Different Kinds Of Wildlife

Very unexpectedly, a whale was beached at Stepney (in 1309), having made its way along a busy – and murky – Thames.

Bat boxes are provided alongside the East End's canals, and bats can be seen in Mile End Park and Victoria Park, along with a profusion of moths, butterflies and squirrels.

The Ecology Park, part of Mile End Park, has an array of moths, spiders, dragonflies, and damselflies.

Grey seals have been regularly spotted in recent years in the river around the Isle of Dogs, West India Quay, and Millwall Docks, perhaps attracted by the cast-offs from Billingsgate Fish Market. Porpoise and dolphin have also been seen around West India Dock and Heron Quay.

Anglers have caught carp weighing up to 25lb in Victoria Park Lake, with smaller examples being landed in the Blackwall Basin, which is also the place to catch bream, perch, pike and roach. Eels can be found in local waterways, but whitebait – once caught in shoals at Blackwall for consumption at annual whitebait dinners – are no longer as much in evidence. Shadwell Basin is also the place for carp, bream and roach. Fishing on the River Lea dates back to at least the seventeenth century, and no doubt long before.

Buglife spotters in the East End can expect to see seven-spot ladybirds, buff-tailed bumble bees, hairy dragon flies, marmalade hover flies, and hawthorn shield bugs – among others – along the banks of the Thames.

SOME FLORAL FACTS

The first fuchsia sold in England was by a sailor, returned from the West Indies, at the Prospect of Whitby (Wapping) in exchange for a quarter of a pint of rum (1780).

Columbia Road flower market in Bethnal Green is London's most sweet-smelling market. Every Sunday, dozens and dozens of stalls fill the surrounding streets with floral fragrance.

The ability to bring exotic plants from overseas was originally thanks to Whitechapel's Nathaniel Ward, who invented the terrarium in about 1830. Although trained as a doctor, he had found seedlings flourished better using airtight glass than in the polluted East End air, generating plenty of excitement in gardening circles at the time. Crucially, it also meant that trees and seedlings could be sent safely overseas, so quinine-bearing trees (cinchona), for example, could be sent to countries with malaria.

Rare orchids can be seen at the Ecology Park, part of Mile End Park.

MORE THAN COCKNEY SPARROWS

From the seventeenth century (possibly even earlier) to the nineteenth century, the Green Goose Fair took place every Whitsun at Bow (now Fairfield Road area), featuring ready-roasted fowl. Contemporary wits were known to point out that a green goose was also a slang term for a cuckold or harlot! The drunken and rowdy behaviour of the crowds were the main reason for its final closure.

The nineteenth-century Bird Fair in Club Row, Shoreditch, was described in an issue of *Penny Illustrated* dated 19 April 1873 as:

> 'a mingled hubbub of sounds [including] cackling geese, clucking fowls, singing birds, yelping dogs, the clattering of horses' hooves, the whistling and shouting of men, with a chorus from sherbet-sellers, cake and fruit vendors, dealers in ginger-beer and groundsel, periwinkles and potatoes [and] sparrows transformed into canaries [these extraordinary specimens] caught on Hackney Marshes but so disguised as to be sold as just brought over by a sailor from Timbuctoo.'

The houses of Spitalfields weavers in the nineteenth century had bird traps on the roofs. It seems they were famed for their 'skill' in catching song birds – although setting a trap does not sound like too rare a skill.

The Troxy Cinema in Commercial Road once featured live vultures in the foyer as an added 'attraction'.

More recently, in 1981, Grog, one of the Tower of London's ravens, escaped after 21 years' 'service' and was last spotted outside the Rose and Punchbowl in Redmans Road, Whitechapel (now demolished). He was heralded in the press as 'the last traitor' because of the legend that, 'If the Tower of London ravens are lost or fly away, the Crown will fall and Britain with it.'

Twentieth-century birds spotted in . . . Tower Hamlets Cemetery Park include tawny owls, stock doves, spotted flycatchers and bullfinches.

. . . Bromley-by-Bow include black-headed and black-backed gulls, Eurasian blackbirds, European robins, greater spotted woodpeckers, song thrushes, common chaffinches.

. . . East India Dock include grey herons, arctic terns, blue tits, collared doves, mallards, moorhens, mute swans, oystercatchers, common sandpipers, coots, cormorants, greenfinches, pied wagtails, sparrow hawks, sand martins, ring-necked parakeets, grey wagtails, house martins, swallows, willow warblers, jays, kestrels, kingfishers and the black redstart, one of Britain's rarest birds (the latter, incidentally, attracted to Canary Wharf by the carder bee – the bee burrows into the sediments in the shale of the Cabot Tower roof garden). Note that East India Dock Basin, complete with a rare section of salt marsh, is now a nature reserve, on the remains of the once grand East India Docks.

The Cockney Sparrow Project was launched at the Peabody Estate in Whitechapel in August 2009. The project involves Peabody residents creating the ideal habitat for sparrows, swifts, house martins and other wildlife on the estate.

EXCEPTIONAL EAST END WEATHER

On New Year's Eve 1323, a series of damaging floods covered 100 acres of what was then described as Stepney. The flooding left behind a breach in the river wall, which didn't help with subsequent rises in the tide. In fact, 100 years later (1448), as much as 1,000 acres were under water. The lord of the shrinking manor was not a happy man.

During the winter of 1777/8, the Thames froze from Shadwell to Putney. The Frost Fair on the ice was even bigger than on previous occasions and included a travelling menagerie of 'beasts'.

Hurricanes were reported to have had an adverse effect in the East End in 1884. One man was severely injured by the fall of a 60ft wall in Dock Street, Whitechapel, and another was killed and two people injured when a portion of Mann & Crossman's wall blew down into Bath Street (also Whitechapel). In Whitechapel High Street, a man was blown under a tramcar by the severity of the wind, and the wheels passed over him, leaving him with severe injuries.

The exceptionally cold spell in February 1895 resulted in an ice-bound River Thames. The barges and lighters, the working boats, were trapped, causing a financial burden for those who earned their livelihood on the river.

While London often had dense fogs (Pea Soupers) in the nineteenth century, one in 1952 (on 5 December, lasting several days) had a particularly profound effect, and is described by some as the nation's worst single air pollution disaster. On the Isle of Dogs, visibility was down to zero, and people were said to have had difficulty seeing their own feet.

FOUR-LEGGED FRIENDS

Cats

Dick Whittington's famous cat is linked with the coal barges that he owned on the River Lea – known as the Black Cats. They were unloaded near St Mary's Church, Bromley-by-Bow.

When Christopher Smart, the eighteenth-century poet, was admitted to Kirby's Castle (formerly Bethnal House, now Bethnal Green Library – although tricky to pin down for sure) as an insane but 'curable' patient, he was accompanied by his pet which became – for a while – the most famous cat in English literature. Jeffry (or Jeoffrey), was immortalised in a poem about his (the cat's) relationship with God, when he was described as counteracting 'the powers of darkness by his electrical skin and glaring eyes.'

When St Katharine's Dock was built in the 1820s, 300 cats were installed as rat catchers. Additionally, men were paid £1 to clear ships of rats, with 2*d* for each live rat they caught – but it is not clear what happened to the live rats.

Dogs

A troupe of performing dogs (and seven horses) were killed in a fire at Rosemary Branch Gardens in 1852, on the Shoreditch boundary. They were part of a travelling circus, performing in what rivalled the West End's Vauxhall Gardens.

In the nineteenth century, one of the most famous dogs in the area was an 'exhibit' at one of the penny gaffs in Whitechapel. His forefeet had been split to look like lion's claws, and spectators oohed and aahed at what then passed as entertainment.

Since 1912, sculptures of the Dogs of Alcibiades (a fourth-century Athenian statesman) have stood either side of the Sewardstone Road end of Victoria Park. They are copies of a second-century Roman statue held at the British Museum, but have been very badly vandalised over the years, and are now hardly recognisable.

The statue of the Blind Beggar's dog (and his master) have been moved a few times, most recently inhabiting Cranbrook Estate, Roman Road (listed Grade II 1998). The ballad commemorating the fifteenth-century legend suggests that he was not a beggar at all, but Simon de Montfort, a rich aristocrat who wanted to avoid his daughter marrying a fortune-chaser. By posing as a beggar, having been blinded during the Hundred Years War, he and young nubile Bessy were able to sort the genuine from the gold-diggers and the lucky suitor got quite a surprise when his Bethnal Green-born fiancée turned out to be an heiress and not a barmaid (or worse). The Blind Beggar's house, incidentally, is rumoured to be the same as that of William Ryder, a friend of Samuel Pepys.

Another statue of doggy interest is outside the public baths in East India Dock Road. This is the dog accompanying Sir Richard Green, the Blackwall shipbuilder and philanthropist. Sir Richard's dog (the statue that is) has just one ear, the other having been removed by the fire service when they rescued a young lad who had got himself jammed between pet and master.

In 1940, a scruffy and starving stray terrier was taken in by Air Raid Warden King on duty in Poplar. Adopted by the team in Southill Street, he was christened Rip and became their mascot and (unofficial) search dog, the first of his kind. His ability to locate bodies in the aftermath of air raids was instinctive, and he 'served' for five years, saving numerous lives. In July 1945, he was awarded the PDSA Dickin Medal or Blue Cross Medal of the Dumb Friends' League (the animals' Victoria Cross) for, specifically, his work during the Blitz – but, sadly, he only survived another year. His medal was sold at auction in 2009 for a record £24,250.

The Kennel Club organised their Best of British Companion Dog Show at West India Quay to celebrate the 150th anniversary of dog showing in July 2009. Among the winners was Burnsfield, a Jack Russell owned by Denis Glackin from Poplar, who collected first prize for the Waggiest Tail.

Horse stories
In about 1601, a performing horse by the name of Morocco carried the notorious Moll Cutpurse (Queen of Thieves) to Shoreditch from Charing Cross to win her a £20 bet. She was dressed in her favoured men's attire as part of the bet, for which she was condemned to do penance at the south wall of St Paul's Cathedral, to no effect.

In the eighteenth century, the Pound Keeper of Mile End Pound (corner of Mile End Road and what is now Cambridge Heath Road) paid a reward of 1*s* for each horse (or mare, ox or cow) 'captured'

and brought in, and would also charge the owner who came to claim his 'lost' property. Owners often left their horses here after a long journey, and took the Hackney coach to London, which cost around 1s 6d. Was this the first park and ride?

A mare called White Stockings, stolen by Dick Turpin from Epping, was stabled at the Red Lion (now demolished), Colchester Street, Aldgate, in 1738 awaiting collection by his partner-in-crime Tom King. But King arrived at the same time as a constable, and was shot by Turpin in the ensuing confusion.

A few years later, Cooper Thornhill, publican of the Bell Inn in Stilton, Cambridgeshire, wagered 500 guineas that he could ride from Stilton to London and back and return to London in less than fifteen hours (over 213 miles). He did it, ending up at Shoreditch church in 12 hours 17 minutes. Hopefully more than one horse was involved.

MORE ANIMAL TALES

A huge ox was reared on the Isle of Dogs (Old Tun Marsh) for five years until it reached 236 stone. In 1720, it was sold at Leadenhall Market in the City for 100 guineas, the largest sold in England.

The first – possibly the only – goat to twice circumnavigate the globe died in Mile End in April 1772. The goat had travelled with Captains Wallis (HMS *Dolphin*) and Cook (HMS *Endeavour*), the latter associated with this area. It was a shame that the goat died before being able to take up its retirement privileges as a 'pensioner of Greenwich Hospital', granted by the Lord of the Admiralty!

When a gang attacked a Spitalfields silk warehouse in 1818, they used a bullock as a battering ram. The workers defended themselves with boiling water and shotguns, so, not surprisingly, the bullock ran amok before keeling over – dead.

A fire at the East London Menagerie and Aquarium in Shoreditch High Street, possibly started in the waxworks (1884), resulted in the deaths of all the monkeys, a wolf, a lion cub, a Russian bear and two civet cats with one lioness put down because of the severity of her injuries. Luckier animals included a seal, a jackal, an elk, and three other bears, which were taken to a local stable.

In the nineteenth century, a donkey was known as a Whitechapel brougham, especially if it was pulling a barrow.

A waiter in Commercial Road in April 1899 did not expect to be hospitalised following a goring by a 'mad' cow, but that's what happened when the animal escaped from a nearby drover en route to a dairy yard in Fairclough Street. The escaped cow caused havoc – knocking down a young boy and wrecking a dairy in Mansell Street – and finally had to be restrained by strong ropes in Arrow Alley.

Of the 253 cowsheds in London in 1905, forty were in Stepney. As late as 1938, Cave Brothers in Jubilee Street had forty-five cows supplying milk to local families.

Until the twentieth century, anyone wanting to buy a domestic pet, or a wild animal supplied by a seafarer, could get what they wanted at Jamrach's Emporium on Ratcliff Highway. The wild animals were kept in cages in nearby Betts Street – including monkeys, orangutans, alligators, elephants (£300 in 1875) and lions (£80 in 1913). One of Jamrach's customers was said to be P.T. Barnum, the American showman. There is a story of a Bengal tiger escaping from the store and seizing a small boy – with optional versions of the outcome. The happy outcome is that the boy was rescued by Charles Jamrach who forced his bare hands into the tiger's throat, forcing the animal to drop the boy. The sad version is that the attempt to save him – by dint of striking the tiger with a crowbar – resulted in the boy's death. A statue remains in memory of the incident at the entrance to Tobacco Dock.

When the Columbia Estate in Bethnal Green was built at the end of the nineteenth century, it seems that the doors provided were too small for their frames – a new form of ventilation, perhaps? However, stables were included, not for horses, but for the donkeys belonging to the costermongers. The funding for the stables – and for the whole estate – came from Angela Burdett-Coutts of the Coutts banking family, who also funded horse and cattle drinking troughs in Victoria Park. She did so much for the East End that her funeral in 1907 included costermongers, pearly kings and queens and flower girls as well as royalty.

The first dispensary for sick animals was founded by Maria Dickin in Whitechapel in 1917, moving soon after to Harford Street, Mile End, with a hospital following in Commercial Road. This was the modest beginnings of the PDSA.

At the start of the Canary Wharf development, a flock of sheep from Mudchute Farm (and a swarm of bees) were let loose into the audience by local residents as a form of protest. It certainly attracted the attention they were looking for.

When neighbours of the Bethnal Green owner of Mimi, the 10-stone Vietnamese pot-bellied pig, complained in 2008 about the smell, noise and flies, she ended up in a superior dwelling as part of the Mudchute Farm on the Isle of Dogs. Residents of Blythendale House, Mansford Street, were delighted.

11

WATERWAYS, RAILWAYS & OTHER WAYS

CAPERING AROUND THE CANALS

The River Lea Act of 1766 authorised the construction of London's oldest canal, which became known as the Limehouse Cut. It started out in 1770 as the Poplar Canal, a straight section linking the Rivers Lea and Thames. In 1968, its exit lock to the Thames was replaced by a length of canal linking the cut with the Regent's Canal Dock now known as Limehouse Basin, the gateway to over 2,000 miles of navigable waterways. The cut was originally built for sailing barges, but can, of recent years, be accessed – innovatively – by floating pontoons. A later cut connected the River Lea between Old Ford and Leyton, known as the Hackney Cut.

The third canal to be built in London was on the Isle of Dogs, opened in December 1805, and originally called the City Canal. Although technically a short cut, it was sometimes quicker to sail round the Isle of Dogs if the tides were on your side, so it was sold and subsequently rebuilt: the remaining expanse of water is now known as South Dock and is managed by British Waterways.

In July 2009, the first punts to be licensed on the canal by British Waterways started operating between Mile End Lock, Old Ford Lock and Top End Lock (on the Hertford Union Canal). This enterprise was the brainchild of a medical student at Queen Mary College (Mile End).

WATER POWER AND WIND

In 1598, John Stow wrote about Wapping Mill (part of Wapping Ness) in the thirteenth century, near another mill in Shadwell, at Bell Wharf, both tide mills using river power to grind corn for the City of London. He also wrote of another mill 'with two wheels, known as

Crash Mills' which had stood at the bottom of Nightingale Lane (now Thomas More Street, Wapping).

Prior to the outbreak of Civil War, there was a windmill at Whitechapel. However, it was rendered useless when a massive fort-like defence was constructed in the vicinity. This remained as Whitechapel Mount, until the development of the London Hospital.

The three eighteenth-century mills which gave their name to Three Mill Lane were originally built for grinding corn (for flour) but later became distilleries. The Clock Mill and the House Mill remain, the latter believed to be the largest tidal mill still in existence in the world. It was used during the First World War to grind corn and chestnuts to make ingredients for explosives and was the last watermill in Britain to be used to produce flour – and gin.

A nineteenth-century mill, the Wheatsheaf, was a significant part of the McDougall's self-raising flour production business at Millwall. It was the only building in the area to survive the Blitz in the Second World War, but didn't survive the developers of the 1980s.

SHINING LIGHTS

London's only lighthouse is at Trinity Buoy Wharf situated at the mouth of the River Lea (Orchard Place), and dating from 1864. Records of another, earlier, lighthouse (demolished between the wars) show that Michael Faraday was among its earliest scientific advisers as this lighthouse was not used for navigation; it was known as the Experimental Lighthouse, and also used to train lighthouse keepers. It was Faraday's experiments that prepared the way for the first electric powered lighthouse at Dover. The lighthouse was reborn in the twenty-first century as a sound installation, continuing its experimental heritage. The adjoining Chain and Buoy Store (the largest of the surviving on-site Victorian structures) has a specially strengthened floor below the roof space because of the weight of Faraday's equipment.

A Variety Of Passengers

While the first voluntary passengers for Australia left from Dunbar Wharf, Limehouse, by steamer, the earlier involuntary ones (the convicts) left from Wapping Old Stairs.

Some of the first successful English settlers left from Brunswick Wharf (Blackwall) to found a plantation at Jamestown in Virginia, named after King James who had authorised the whole project. They arrived four months later (in April 1607) in three merchant ships: the *Susan Constant*, the *Godspeed* and the *Discovery*. The most famous of these settlers was Captain John Smith, saved in legend by Pocahontas. Less well known was John Laydon, a carpenter, who married in 1609 and fathered the first child from a Virginia marriage, baptised, a little predictably, Virginia.

And A Variety Of Vessels

Before mills appeared at Millwall, it was the base for the earliest recorded Thames ferry east of the City of London, which plied between Millwall and Greenwich in the middle of the fifteenth century.

The first ship to be built and launched in Limehouse was in 1586, believed to be the *Greyhound*.

One of the earliest frigates, the *Constant Warwick*, was built for the Royal Navy at Ratcliff in 1645, along with other warships.

HMS *Bounty* of mutiny fame was an old collier purchased by the Admiralty at Wapping Old Stairs. It was fitted out for its eighteenth-century voyage to the Pacific in order to obtain breadfruit to feed slaves in Britain's Caribbean colonies.

The SS *Great Eastern*, the largest ship at the time (four times bigger than any other), was designed by Isambard Kingdom Brunel with a double iron hull, one inside the other. It was launched in January 1858 from Millwall. To give some idea of the scale, 3,000,000 rivets were used, driven by 200 rivet gangs. At 690ft it was too long for the river, and had to be launched sideways, ending up with launch costs of some £120,000. Due to these difficulties, it was the last big ship to be built on the Isle of Dogs, but the remains of the timber slipway built for the purpose can still be seen on the foreshore near West Ferry Road. Note that the *Great Eastern*, although damaged by an explosion on its maiden voyage, laid the first Atlantic telecommunications cable.

In 1860, the Royal Navy's first ironclad warship, HMS *Warrior* (supposedly the largest and fastest warship in the world), was launched at the Thames Ironworks – between Bow Creek and the East India Dock basin – reducing the injuries to gun crews caused by flying wood fragments during battle. Among other famous vessels, they had also launched the SS *Himalaya* for P&O a few years earlier, briefly the world's largest passenger ship before being sold to the Admiralty. Thames Ironworks was the most important shipbuilder on the Thames, and the biggest private shipbuilder in the country – although they extended their brief when necessary, e.g. supplying iron for such projects as Blackfriars Bridge. They were less successful when launching the *Albion* for the Admiralty in 1898: so many thousands of spectators turned up that the huge wave caused by the vessel's launch smashed the slipway to bits – with thirty-eight drowning as a result.

This was the first ship launched by a member of the royal family, the Duchess of York, but was, perhaps surprisingly after that experience, not the last. Thames Ironworks' last ship was the *Thunderer*, launched in 1912, the year the company ran out of orders in spite of the efforts of the disabled Arnold Hills, its principal director, renowned for his vegetarian, teetotal, anti-smoking lifestyle. Incidentally, the works' football club became West Ham United in 1900, the hammers of their emblem representing riveting hammers.

The Samuda Brothers (Joseph and Jacob) at Bow Creek built dozens of warships between 1843 and 1890 but not only for the Royal Navy – also for the Germans and Japanese. In fact, there is some evidence to support a visit by Japanese Admiral Togo Heihachiro (the 'Nelson of the East') in 1877 for work experience while studying in the UK. However, Jacob Samuda did not live to see their success – he, and six crew, were killed on their first experimental trip in the *Gypsy Queen* (near Blackwall) in November 1844 when a boiler full of scalding water burst.

The *Duke of Northumberland*, the world's first steam lifeboat, launched in 1888, was also built at Blackwall – by R. & H. Green. During the nineteenth century, nearly 90 per cent of the RNLI's lifeboats were built by local shipbuilders (including Thames Ironworks).

The fastest vessels in the Navy were the torpedo boats built by Yarrow's yard on the Isle of Dogs (*c.* 1887), just a few years after Yarrow's had supplied the Russians with similar vessels. Yarrow's were also responsible for David Livingstone's boat, the *Ilala*, and for other vessels used in Stanley's exploration of the Congo and General Gordon's expedition along the Nile. According to an 1884 issue of *The Graphic*, one of these, a small steamer christened *Le Stanley*, had to be taken to pieces at the point where the Congo became un-navigable and then carried up country before being put back together again – a feat requiring 500 natives.

The RRS *Discovery*, famous for carrying Captain Scott to the Antarctic, was laid up at East India Dock in 1920, and was used as the headquarters of the 16th Stepney Scout Group until 1922.

OTHER WAYS OF WORKING ON THE RIVER

There is a sculpture outside Ensign House, Marsh Wall, on the Isle of Dogs, which salutes all the river workers: toshers (who scavenged in the mud and sewage for anything, i.e. any tosh, they could sell), bargees, aletasters, coalheavers, dockers and ferrymen. Mudlarks – mainly children – were also prevalent until the 1920s, collecting anything thrown up by the tide.

The River Police first patrolled the crowded River Thames from their headquarters at Wapping New Stairs in 1798.

NAUTICAL NOTES

Sir Thomas Spert 'of Stepney' was the first master of Trinity House, set up in 1514 to supervise lighthouses and river pilots. He was buried at St Dunstan's, Stepney, in 1541.

In 1794, a fire broke out at Clove's barge builders in Ratcliff. One barge loaded with saltpetre, once ignited, set off a series of explosions destroying hundreds of private houses, more than thirty warehouses, and several ships on the river. The resulting 1,000 homeless were temporarily housed in 150 tents on Stepney Fields (by St Dunstan's Church). This would seem to have been the worst fire disaster since the Great Fire of London.

The East India Company, based in Blackwall, became the most powerful commercial concern in British history, with most of its first seafarers from Stepney and Ratcliff. Its shipbuilding yards were opened to construct East Indiamen vessels, which were armed as warships. Its fate was sealed by the Indian mutiny of 1857–8.

Among those who picked up trophies at the annual Doggett's Coat and Badge Race (a race for lightermen and watermen from London to Chelsea bridges) was Robert Burwood from Wapping, who won first prize in 1874. Others who achieved temporary fame included two of the six rowers in the 1904 final: W. Gobbett from Poplar, who came second, and H. Macfarlane from Stepney, sixth.

BREAKING RECORDS UNDER THE RIVER

The first tunnel constructed underneath a navigable river anywhere in the world was built under the Thames between 1825 and 1843 by Marc Brunel. It connects Wapping with Rotherhithe. Queen Victoria opened the 400-yard tunnel, the construction of which had resulted in the deaths of at least ten workers who contracted such diseases as typhoid from the polluted river and putrid air. Within twenty-four hours, 50,000 people had walked along its length at one penny a time. Once the novelty had worn off, in 1852, the first Thames Tunnel Fancy Fair took place here with sword swallowers, fire eaters, coconut shies and even steam organs. The tunnel was sold to the East London Railway in 1865 for £200,000, electrified in 1913, and is still in use as part of the tube line between Wapping and Rotherhithe. During its refurbishment in 2010, when the East London line was being extended, there was another opportunity to walk its length – and the first to do so was Boris Johnson, followed by the band of the Coldstream Guards.

In 1897, the longest underwater crossing in the world was constructed to link Blackwall with East Greenwich. It had taken some five years to construct, with six people killed during the work. Its 6,200ft were designed for horse-drawn traffic, and it was the only free road crossing available to such traffic between Tower Bridge and the Woolwich Ferry, 9 miles away. Blackwall Tunnel had electric lighting, unlike the rest of Poplar, which meant it needed its own power station. The original 1897 plan was to have two tunnels, but the second was not built until 1967.

Bridging Continents

The Victoria Bridge over the St Lawrence River at Montreal, Canada, was built with ironwork made at Robert Baillie's yard in Blackwall in the 1850s, and designed by Robert Stephenson who built the Blackwall railway. Baillie's also provided the giant tubes for the Britannia Bridge over the Menai Strait, a tad closer to home. Over half a century later, as Westwood, Baillie & Co., they erected parts of the Sukkur Bridge over the Indus River in what is now Pakistan – at the time, this was the world's largest cantilevered bridge.

Dock Data

The West India Dock on the Isle of Dogs opened in 1802, with space for 600 ships. This was one of the greatest civil engineering projects of its day, with 54 acres of water divided into import and export docks. Between 1802 and the abolition of slavery in 1807, over seventy ships sailed from the dock to West Africa, resulting in the purchase and transportation of nearly 25,000 enslaved Africans, with over 3,000 not surviving the journey. The dock closed in 1980.

The first enclosed docks in London were opened in 1805 at Wapping (the London Docks) on drained marshland, known centuries earlier as Wapping on the Woze (i.e. drain). The first ship to enter the 90 acres of the new London Dock was *The London Packet*. Wapping Docks closed in 1968.

East India Dock was opened soon after – in 1806 on the Isle of Dogs. This originally served the East India Company's trading interests but was defunct by 1967.

The Regent's Canal Dock (1820–1969), joining the canal to the Thames (now Limehouse Basin), was one of the first docks to use hydraulic power, from the pumping station at Commercial Road locks.

Before St Katharine's Dock was opened (1828) it took between eight and fourteen days to unload a 350-ton ship (depending on the season), but by 1850 a 500-ton ship could be unloaded in just a couple of days because the warehouses were close enough to the ships to allow cranes to unload straight from ship to warehouse. The construction of this dock meant that 11,000 people lost their homes (with only the landlords compensated) and the Royal Hospital of St Katharine had to be moved to Regent's Park in central London. The dock is now a marina.

In 1868, Millwall Docks was added linking up with West India Dock in the 1920s, and lasting until 1980. These docks housed the first purpose-built granary for the Baltic grain market – since demolished. Note that the additional Royal Docks were further east, outside the scope of this listing.

By the middle of the nineteenth century, more than 10,000 dockers were employed in East London. The demise of these local docks had a whole range of causes, not least the demand for larger vessels and the absence of railway links.

WHARFS AND WATERWORKS

In the mid-1860s, the East London Waterworks Company allowed unfiltered water into the water supply from the River Lea, prompting a cholera epidemic. Therefore beer became even more popular than usual, because it was safe – and cheaper even than tea which was heavily taxed at the time. Most of London's water still comes from the Lea and the Thames.

Bow Wharf in Grove Road was originally a Victorian glue factory (and more recently enjoyed a very different lifestyle as home to Jongleurs Comedy Club).

Brunswick Cattle Wharf, Blackwall, had a slaughterhouse attached, convenient for the mixed cargoes of sheep and cattle that were unloaded there. By the end of the nineteenth century, rules of hygiene and safety and animal welfare put an end to such 'conveniences'.

EARLY FORMS OF WATERY TRANSPORT

There was a ferry from the Isle of Dogs to Greenwich which dated from at least the sixteenth century, and is mentioned by Samuel Pepys in his diary. Watermen and ferries took passengers across the Thames until the nineteenth century, because London Bridge was the only option as a pedestrian route across the river until Tower Bridge opened in 1894. There was also a steamer service operating from Blackwall by the nineteenth century.

MORE WAYS OF GETTING AROUND

In the eighteenth century, stagecoaches ran between Romford (Essex) and Whitechapel, with a return fare of 1s 3d for those who could face the elements outside or 2s 2d inside. By 1825, there were as many as seventy-two return stagecoach journeys running every day between Blackwall and the City of London.

A few ballooning trials took place in the area – one, on 26 May 1825, started from the gardens of the Golden Eagle, Mile End. The balloonist, Mr Graham, had arranged a firework display to mark the occasion, but the rain put a dampener on the event. Another (unidentified) aeronaut got cold feet after planning an ascent from the Globe Pleasure Gardens (1844) and sent up a bewigged straw dummy in his place. Professional aeronaut, Henry Coxwell (1819–1900), did rather better, making a reputed 1,000-plus ascents, at least one of them from Spring Gardens, Stepney Green (now Spring Walk) and one from Globe Pleasure Gardens (now Whitman Road, Mile End).

A horse bus service operated through Blackwall Tunnel at the end of the nineteenth century, linking Poplar with Deptford in South London. This necessitated the employment of an army of small boys to keep the roadway inside the tunnel clear of horse dung. Less than thirty years later, horses had been replaced by buses (at a fare of 2*d*).

A tram system operated through the East End from 1870 with a 4-mile route from Whitechapel through to Bow Church and West Ham at 1*d* a mile, with a minimum fare of 2*d*. This was extended to Aldgate in 1871, and, two years later, an additional tram route covered the area between Poplar and Bloomsbury in central London via Limehouse and Spitalfields. These trams had a speed limit of 9mph. Horse-drawn trams ceased during the First World War when the horses were needed for war duty.

A foot tunnel 50ft beneath the Thames was constructed to link the Isle of Dogs with Greenwich in 1902, and is now part of the UK's National Cycle Route. However, you have to push the bike through the tunnel rather than ride it.

Trolley buses were running in the East End by 1940 and diesel buses were introduced by the 1960s.

When the Limehouse Link opened in 1993, it was Britain's (or, according to *Construction News*, Europe's) most expensive stretch of road, costing over £255,000,000 for just 1.8km.

Pedicabs (London rickshaws) started operating in Canary Wharf in March 2004, after their success in the West End of London. They are environmentally friendly, nippy, fun – and eccentric!

TRAIN OR STRAIN?

The Eastern Counties Railway opened a railway line from Mile End (Devonshire Street) to Romford in 1839, and a year later the London to Blackwall railway opened (thanks to the Stephensons) initially using long cables at each end until they were replaced by engines.

The North London Railway (from the mid-nineteenth century) had its works and depot in Campbell Road and Devons Road (Bow) respectively. The last steam locomotives left Devons Road in 1958, and it became the first all-diesel depot in London.

When the viaduct carrying the branch line of the London to Blackwall railway (near where Island Gardens station on the Isle of Dogs is now) was built in 1871, steam trains were not allowed to travel through the docks. It was feared that sparks from the engine could start a fire, and the trains had to be horse-drawn.

The extended East London tube line which connects East London with South London is due to open in 2011.

The Dapper Docklands Light Railway

The UK's only driverless automatically operated passenger railway opened in 1987 linking the Isle of Dogs with the City of London. The system, which took some three years to construct, looks like a monorail but at ground level, and has a speed of around 50mph. It started – at a cost of £77,000,000 – with thirteen stations but is gradually being extended into the City, South London, and further into East London.

The viaduct over the Regent's Canal at Limehouse Basin (formerly known as the Regent's Canal Dock) was built in 1839 by George and Robert Stephenson, with trains pulled across by cables. It was the first railway to be controlled by an electric telegraph system, and is still used by the DLR.

The Secret Railway

For 75 years, the Post Office underground railway (built in 1911) linked Whitechapel to Paddington in central London, carrying some four million letters a day in computer-controlled trains. The length of the journey, with nine stops, was just 26 minutes – faster than the underground used for passengers.

The Train That Lost Its Way

The last North London Railway locomotive in service was built at Bow Works in 1880. Its original brief covered shunting in the London Docks but the engine was for many years part of the NLR. However, in 1931 it spent several years well away from home, working on the steep Cromford and High Peak Railway in Derbyshire, until being withdrawn. The Bluebell Railway then stepped in, rescuing the vehicle in 1962 and giving it a total overhaul in the 1980s. Ready for another overhaul, it can now be seen in the locomotive shed at Sheffield Park station in Sussex, awaiting its refurbishment.

Lost East End Stations

Victoria Park was opened in 1856 and demolished in 1957 after years of closure, with a second later location nearby closing in the 1940s – although the very last traces, the junction points, were not removed until 1984.

Globe Road station opened in 1884 and closed for good in 1916, a time when many stations closed, often temporarily, due to lack of staff with so many men serving in the First World War.

Leman Street station (dating from 1877) closed in 1941 due to declining passenger numbers. Though surely the decline may have had something to do with the fact that there was a war on.

Coborn Road station opened in 1865 on the site of the original Old Ford station becoming 'Coborn Road (Old Ford)' in 1879. It was resited and went through a few spells of closure before finally closing in 1946. A bricked-up archway, once the main entrance, is all that remains.

Confusingly, there were two Shoreditch stations. One, on the East London railway, opened in 1876, later becoming part of the London tube network, and closed in 2006. The other, on the North London Railway, dates from 1869, and was closed in October 1940.

Poplar East India Road station opened on 1 August 1866, but was demolished in 1947 after being badly damaged during the Second World War.

Bow railway station opened in 1850, although it seems to have been rebuilt in 1870 in such a fanciful style that the building was subsequently used as a concert hall and a *palais de danse*. A fire finished it off in 1956 although the lines had not been used since 1944.

St Mary's station, Whitechapel, closed in 1938 and was pretty much demolished in the 1940 Blitz. It had become superfluous to requirements once Aldgate East station had been moved further east.

Cannon Street Road station survived for just a few years in the nineteenth century (1842–8). It probably seemed like a good idea at the time. Others have been reborn, e.g. the site of the old Millwall Dock station is now Crossharbour station on the DLR.

And A Remarkable Find

When Euston station's Victorian edifice was replaced in the 1960s, its elaborate – and hefty – entrance arch was used to plug a hole in the bed of the River Lea. Thirty years later, half of the arch with its distinctive gold lettering ('Euston') became apparently clearly visible to Dan Cruickshank (the journalist – and Spitalfields resident) and his team when making an episode of *One Foot in the Past*. The arch may one day be restored and Cruickshank no doubt has plans for the remaining 50 per cent presumably still hidden under the murky waters.

12

ON THIS DAY

1 January 1922	Minnie Lansbury died of pneumonia following her imprisonment over the Poplar rates dispute.
2 January 1608	Christopher Newport, the Limehouse mariner, reached Jamestown, Virginia.
3 January 1911	Siege of Sidney Street (with Winston Churchill in attendance).
4 January 1642	Weaver and prophet Richard Farnham, who had died of plague, was buried at St Mary's, Whitechapel.
5 January 2006	George Galloway, MP for Bethnal Green and Bow, turned up on Channel 4's *Celebrity Big Brother*.
6 January 1937	Local fascists smashed up the premises of the Whitechapel and St George's Young Communists' League.
7 January 1928	Tidal surge left widespread flooding on the Isle of Dogs.
8 January 2009	The Monteverdi Choir put on a concert for 176 children from Tower Hamlets at Christ Church, Spitalfields.
9 January 1799	James Eyers convicted of the murder of Gabriel Franks at Wapping.
10 January 1885	Toynbee Hall formally opened (near Aldgate East).
11 January 2002	East End drama *Last Orders* opened in UK cinemas.
12 January 1932	Des O'Connor born in Stepney.
13 January 1842	Birth of Sir Alfred Yarrow, the Isle of Dogs shipbuilder.
14 January 1902	Anti-immigration demonstration at the People's Palace, Mile End Road.
15 January 2010	Annual Ice Sculpting Festival took place at Canada Square Park, Canary Wharf, the first time at this location.

16 January 1861	Dock labourers broke into food shops in Whitechapel in desperation as the heavy frost meant they were not working.
17 January 1863	Death of Sir Richard Green, Blackwall shipbuilder and philanthropist.
18 January 1887	Seventeen people crushed to death in the stampede to exit the Yiddish Theatre, Spitalfields, following (false) alarm of fire.
19 January 1982	Billingsgate Fish Market opened on its new site at West India Docks.
20 January 1669	Susannah Annesley, mother of John Wesley, born in Spital Yard.
21 January 1888	Harry Plunket Greene made his successful singing debut in Handel's *Messiah* at the People's Palace, Mile End.
22 January 1951	Death of Fanny Wilkinson, landscape gardener responsible for the garden at the Geffrye Museum plus Meath Gardens and Bethnal Green Gardens.
23 January 1786	George Combes executed at Execution Dock, Wapping, for the murder of William Allen.
24 January 1986	The Battle of Wapping started – a strike of 6,000 newspaper workers.
25 January 1981	The Limehouse Declaration issued at the home of David Owen in Limehouse, the start of the Social Democratic Party.
26 January 1850	Samuel Gompers born in Spitalfields, the man who emigrated to New York and set up the US version of the TUC.
27 January 1888	Dr Barnardo provided 1,200 hot roast dinners at the Edinburgh Castle Mission Hall, Limehouse.
28 January 1927	Birth of Ronnie Scott, jazz supremo, in the Commercial Road Maternity Unit.
29 January 1734	Murder of Mary Defour by her mother, Judith, both from Bethnal Green workhouse.
30 January 1649	Richard Brandon, East End executioner, beheaded Charles I.
31 January 1858	Brunel's steamship, the *Great Eastern*, launched at Millwall.

1 February 1911	Launch of warship HMS *Thunderer* from Thames Ironworks, Bow Creek.
2 February 2009	Launch of drama series *Whitechapel* on ITV.
3 February 1906	Jewish Anarchists' Club opened in Jubilee Street.
4 February 1850	Frederick Charrington, the teetotal brewery heir, born in Bow Road.
5 February 1646	Baptist preacher Thomas Lambe debated for five hours at Spitalfields regarding the mortality of the soul.
6 February 1919	Louis Heren, war correspondent and *Times* journalist, was born at Shadwell.
7 February 1891	'Brides in the Bath' murderer George Smith, from Bethnal Green, had his first conviction – for stealing a bicycle.
8 February 1792	Death of Wapping female warrior Hannah Snell.
9 February 1996	Docklands bombing by the IRA at (South) Canary Wharf.
10 February 2001	Death of Whitechapel's Abraham Beame, the Mayor of New York City.
11 February 1985	Ronnie Kray married Elaine Mildener while in prison.

12 February 1870	Birth of music hall's Marie Lloyd in Plumber Street, Shoreditch.
13 February 2009	'Bliss' (charity for babies born with problems) set up a world record kissing chain of 165 people at Spitalfields Market.
14 February 1951	The first tenants, the Snoddys, moved into Gladstone House on the new Lansbury Estate in Poplar.
15 February 1986	Police and 5,000 pickets clashed at Wapping to stop the distribution of the *Sun*, *The Times* and the *News of the World*.
16 February 2007	The queen and the Duke of Edinburgh visited Millwall fire station.
17 February 1924	Local boxer Teddy Baldock beat Bill Lewis at Premierland.
18 February 1888	The first Salvation Army hostel opened at 21 West India Dock Road by General William Booth.
19 February 1985	The first episode of *East Enders* was aired on the BBC.
20 February 1838	Lucy Scales and her sister were on the receiving end of 'Spring-Heeled Jack's' reign of terror when walking in Limehouse (a man fond of assuming a terrifying expression before jumping out in front of his 'victims').
21 February 1859	George Lansbury born – Bow politician and leader of the Labour party.
22 February 1869	St Gabriel's Church, Chrisp Street, Poplar, was consecrated.
23 February 1924	'Brilliant' Chang, Limehouse opium dealer, was arrested (and later deported).
24 February 1898	Legendary footballer Walter Tull was placed in Bonner Road orphanage.
25 February 1934	Bernard Bresslaw, the actor, was born in Stepney.
26 February 1854	The first advertisement for Wilton's Music Hall appeared in *The Era*.
27 February 1890	One-time Stepney resident, the Hon. Roland Phillips (or Philipps), Scout Commissioner for Bethnal Green, Stepney and Poplar, was born.

28 February 1874	Wapping's Arthur Orton found guilty of perjury in the Tichborne Trial.
1 March 1970	The Isle of Dogs declared independence!
2 March 1789	Death of Jack Broughton, the Wapping waterman who became heavyweight boxing champion of England.
3 March 1943	173 died at Bethnal Green tube station in a panic over the sound of an air raid siren.
4 March 1969	The Kray twins were found guilty of the murder of Jack 'The Hat' McVitie.
5 March 1894	The 'only American Indian actress, Go-won-go Mohawk' started a one-week performance at the Pavilion Theatre in Whitechapel Road.
6 March 1912	Myer Abramovitch hanged for the murder of local Hanbury Street restaurateurs, Solomon and Annie Milstein.
7 March 1903	Lenin was the main speaker at the New Alexandra Hall, Jubilee Street.
8 March 1750	A relatively minor earthquake hit London and its surrounds, with damage obvious in Whitechapel where several houses were demolished.
9 March 1966	George Cornell was shot by Ronnie Kray in the Blind Beggar.
10 March 1954	Tina 'I love to love' Charles, disco diva, born in London Hospital, Whitechapel.
11 March 1840	Foundation stone laid for Christ Church, Watney Street.
12 March 1838	Birth of Sir William Perkin in Shadwell, renowned chemist.
13 March 2010	Last opportunity to walk from Rotherhithe to Wapping through Brunel's tunnel before underground trains restarted.
14 March 1868	Millwall Docks opened.
15 March 1961	The queen and the Duke of Edinburgh visited Poplar.
16 March 2009	A fire at the Sikh temple in Harley Grove, Bow, destroyed the first floor.
17 March 1995	Ronnie Kray died.

18 March 1857	Gunboat HMS *Jasper* was launched at Blackwall, ending up in the Vampire Fleet, chasing pirates for the Chinese Government.
19 March 2010	Mayor Boris Johnson opened Braham Street Park, Whitechapel.
20 March 1906	Birth of Abraham Beame in Whitechapel (the first Jewish Mayor of New York).
21 March 1942	The start of Warship Week, a Bethnal Green fund-raiser.
22 March 2007	Royal Mail stamp issued to commemorate Granville Sharp, whose meeting with a Wapping slave led in part to abolition of the trade.
23 March 1860	Horatio Bottomley, the financier and fraudster, born in Bethnal Green.
24 March 2007	Protest took place outside Starbucks in Whitechapel Road: Knees Up Against Starbucks.
25 March 1889	Prince Albert Victor opened the Institute for Working Lads, Bethnal Green.
26 March 2010	Sam Webb from the Isle of Dogs won the British light middleweight title.
27 March 1945	The last V2 bomb demolished Hughes Mansions in Vallance Road, killing 130.
28 March 2000	Canada Place retail mall opened at Canary Wharf.
29 March 1772	Emanuel Swedenborg, theologist, died at Wapping.
30 March 1770	The Society of Supporters of the Bill of Rights met at the Mile End Assembly Rooms.
31 March 1888	Betts Street baths opened – to serve 70,000 local residents.
1 April 1918	Isaac Rosenberg, the Stepney poet, killed in combat.
2 April 1873	Queen Victoria visited Victoria Park.
3 April 1999	Death of Lionel Bart, Cockney king of the musical.
4 April 1896	Double murder of John Levy and his housekeeper in Turner Street, during a burglary.
5 April 1935	Peter Grant born in Bethnal Green (Manager of Led Zeppelin).

6 April 2010	Royal London Hospital designated one of the only three trauma centres in London.
7 April 1724	Death of Roger Grant, the Wapping-based oculist to George I.
8 April 1899	Hermann Geeling gored by a rampaging cow in Arrow Alley, Aldgate.
9 April 1937	Dora Creditor, brought up in Stepney (and educated at Coborn School, Bow) married Hugh Gaitskell, who became leader of the Labour party.
10 April 1924	The Duchess of York (later the queen) opened the Docklands settlement.
11 April 1826	The building that started life as the Royalty Theatre, Wellclose Square, burned down.
12 April 1912	Birth of Jack 'Spot' Comer, the King of Aldgate, gangster and racketeer.
13 April 1576	Lease signed by James Burbage for London's first theatre at Shoreditch.
14 April 1842	Catherine Eddowes, a Jack the Ripper victim, born.
15 April 2008	The Bishop of London visited St George-in-the-East in Cannon Street Road for evensong.
16 April 1991	Sir David Lean died at his home in Narrow Street, Limehouse.
17 April 1610	Henry Hudson set off from St Katharine's Dock to find the North-West passage to China.
18 April 1653	Damaris Page, notorious Stepney brothel keeper, married James Dry.
19 April 1763	James Cook left his wife and family in Mile End to set out for Newfoundland.
20 April 1965	Reggie Kray married Frances Shea at St James's, Bethnal Green.
21 April 1814	Birth of Angela Burdett-Coutts, philanthropist behind Bethnal Green's innovative, if unsuccessful, development at Columbia Square.
22 April 1805	The first exhibition by the Society of Painters in Watercolours, founded by Whitechapel-born artist Samuel Shelley.
23 April 2010	The Genesis Cinema, Mile End, was one of those kicking off the start of the annual East End Film Festival.

24 April 2009	The Dickin medal awarded to Rip, the Poplar doggy hero, sold for £24,250.
25 April 2010	A charity football match (for Tribute 2 A Legend Trust) was held at Mile End Stadium: London Amputees v All Stars.
26 April 1915	Stepney's 'Issy' Smith (Shmeilowitz) was the first living recipient of the Victoria Cross for bravery this day at Ypres.
27 April 1759	Mary Wollstonecraft was born in Primrose Street, Spitalfields.
28 April 1772	The death at Mile End of the first goat to circumnavigate the globe.
29 April 1949	Actress Anita Dobson was born in Stepney.
30 April 1924	The Duke and Duchess of York visited the new Docklands settlement.
1 May 1926	Local dockers were among those called out on strike by the TUC.
2 May 1737	Dick Turpin and fellow outlaw Tom (or Matthew) King were ambushed by law officers in the Old Red Lion off Whitechapel High Street.
3 May 2007	Sir Alan Sugar unveiled a supercomputer at Queen Mary College, Mile End.
4 May 1914	The headquarters of the East London suffragettes opened in Old Ford Road, Bethnal Green.
5 May 1928	Queen Mary saw a performance of *Il Pagliacci* by the Oxford House Choral Society at Bethnal Green.
6 May 1935	Mothers of ten babies born today (Jubilee Day) in Poplar were presented with 'perambulators'.
7 May 1940	The Art Deco Tea Pavilion was opened in Victoria Park.
8 May 1968	All three Krays arrested in a dawn raid.
9 May 1855	Shoreditch-born Marie Lloyd made her first stage appearance at the Eagle, a local music hall.
10 May 1553	Sir Hugh Willoughby departed from Ratcliff Stairs with a small fleet in search of the North-East passage.
11 May 1871	Trial of Arthur Orton from Wapping begins – regarding his claim to be Sir Roger Tichborne.

12 May 1888	300 bakers (Jews and Germans united) went on strike and paraded through Stepney to try to implement union conditions.
13 May 1731	Benefit concert took place at Goodman's Fields Theatre for the composer Peter Prelleur from Spitalfields.
14 May 2007	A 250kg Second World War bomb was discovered in Bethnal Green and successfully defused.
15 May 2008	'Jack the Ripper and the East End' opened at the Museum of Docklands.
16 May 1863	44-year-old Elizabeth Stirling, for twenty years the organist at All Saints, Poplar, married her toyboy Frederick Bridge (twenty-two years younger), the choirmaster of St Andrew in the City of London, at St Dunstan's.
17 May 1993	Prime Minister John Major opened new roads the Limehouse Link and the East India Dock Link.
18 May 1651	John Robins (the supposed reincarnation of Christ) and other 'Ranters' apprehended at Shoreditch and tried for blasphemy.
19 May 1885	Paragon Theatre of Varieties opened in Mile End Road.
20 May 1876	The Hebrew Socialist Union was founded at 40 Gun Street, Spitalfields.
21 May 1886	Debut of the song 'Two Lovely Black Eyes' at the Paragon, Mile End, written and performed by local boy Charles Coborn.
22 May 1897	The original Blackwall Tunnel was opened by the Prince and Princess of Wales.
23 May 1701	Captain Kidd was hanged at Execution Dock, Wapping.
24 May 2003	Museum of Docklands opened.
25 May 1935	King George and Queen Mary visited Limehouse Town Hall.
26 May 1972	Actress Patsy Palmer born in Bethnal Green.
27 May 1915	Arthur Alderton from Cyprus Street, Bethnal Green, was one of those who died on board HMS *Princess Irene*, a mine-laying ship that exploded off Sheerness with only one survivor.

28 May 1996	Salman (Sidney) Greenbaum, renowned Stepney-born 'grammarian' responsible for the *Oxford English Grammar*, died.
29 May 1856	The new Victoria Park station took people to and from a firework display to celebrate the end of the Crimean War.
30 May 1723	Darius Humphreys of Whitechapel indicted for stealing a pair of breeches and a snuff box.
31 May 1859	Big Ben, the bell made at the Whitechapel Bell Foundry, rang for the first time.
1 June 2003	Death of Sidney Bloom, creator of Bloom's famous restaurant in Aldgate.
2 June 1780	Mobs burned down RC chapels in Spitalfields as part of the Gordon Riots.
3 June 1648	Royalist insurgents seized Bow Bridge during the second Civil War.
4 June 1879	Illustrator Mable Lucie Attwell was born at 182 Mile End Road.
5 June 1937	Bandleader Lewis Stone from Bethnal Green was married.
6 June 1892	Record number of visits to Victoria Park on a sunny Whitsun holiday: over 300,000.
7 June 1576	Martin Frobisher, the explorer, left Ratcliff Cross Stairs (landing at Baffin Island, Canada).
8 June 1989	The death of political activist Jack Dash, at the London Hospital, Whitechapel.
9 June 1977	Queen Elizabeth visited St Katharine's Dock as part of the Silver Jubilee celebrations.
10 June 1682	Wapping-born buccaneer Bartholomew Sharpe was indicted for piracy (and acquitted on a technicality).
11 June 1971	Stepney-born bandleader/violinist Ambrose died, aged 74.
12 June 1976	Asians marched against racial violence in the East End.
13 June 1917	German Gotha G bombers dropped a bomb on a Poplar nursery school, killing eighteen children.
14 June 1381	Young Richard II was faced with some 60,000 men from Essex and Kent at Mile End during the Peasants' Revolt.

15 June 1895	The birth of the last of the 'slum priests', Joseph Williamson from Poplar, known as Father Joe, who did a lot of work to assist the plight of local prostitutes.
16 June 1888	The People's Palace library was opened by Princess Louise.
17 June 2000	The Green Bridge over Mile End Road opened.
18 June 1899	The Manager of the Foresters' Arms in St Leonard's Road, Poplar, shot himself over money worries.
19 June 2010	The start of the two-day multi-art-form festival at Victoria Park.
20 June 1818	Eugenius Birch (pier-builder extraordinaire) born at Shoreditch.
21 June 1898	Over thirty people died at the launch of the *Albion* when the slipway bridge broke at Blackwall in the presence of the Duchess of York.
22 June 1909	Joe Loss born at Spitalfields.
23 June 1888	Annie Besant exposed the Match Girls' conditions at Bryant & May's Bow factory in *The Link* ('White Slavery in London').
24 June 1872	The Prince and Princess of Wales opened the museum on the corner of Bethnal Green Road.
25 June 1741	The death of Spitalfields composer/musician Pierre Prelleur.
26 June 1951	Peter Cheyney died – the Whitechapel-born novelist.
27 June 1982	Captain Harry Gee landed an aircraft on Heron Quay in a feasibility test.
28 June 1904	Dorset Street in Spitalfields (regarded by many as 'the worst street in London') renamed Duval Street.
29 June 1672	A fire in Wapping burned down the house of Sir William Warren, naval trader and friend of Samuel Pepys.
30 June 1894	Tower Bridge, on the East End border, opened.
1 July 1840	Trains began to use the unfinished Shoreditch terminus.
2 July 1798	The Marine Police started work from their headquarters at Wapping New Stairs.

3 July 1816	Whitechapel boxer 'Dutch Sam' Elias died.
4 July 1845	Dr Barnardo, the saviour of poverty-stricken Stepney schoolboys, was born.
5 July 1888	Three match girls were sacked from Bryant & May for passing on information about their working conditions.
6 July 1840	The London and Blackwall Railway opened to serve the docks.
7 July 1916	The Hon. Roland Phillips, local Scout commissioner, killed in action.
8 July 1776	The Liberty Bell, made in Whitechapel, rang out the US declaration of independence.
9 July 1864	Thomas Briggs found dying on the railway track near Bow station: the first murder on a British train.
10 July 1932	Death of John Scurr, one-time mayor of Poplar, and MP for Mile End.
11 July 1987	Dr Hannah Billig, the Angel of Cable Street, died.
12 July 1888	A huge balloon took off from Poplar Recreation Ground and stayed aloft for 2 hours and 10 minutes (it landed in Sussex).
13 July 1541	William Jerome, the vicar of Stepney, was burned at the stake for heresy.
14 July 1992	Dr Baldev Kaushal, the GP who was the Bethnal Green folk hero of the Blitz, died at his Bethnal Green home.
15 July 1904	The Victoria Model Steamboat Club was founded in Victoria Park.
16 July 1798	Gabriel Franks, part of the new Marine Police Force, was shot dead at Wapping.
17 July 2009	The band Madness celebrated thirty years in music, in Victoria Park.
18 July 2009	The Kennel Club held their Best of British Companion Dog Show at West India Quay.
19 July 1843	Brunel's SS *Great Britain* launched from Wapping dock.

20 July 1907	The East End Mission opened in Commercial Road.
21 July 2005	A bomb attack on a London bus outside St Leonard's Church, Shoreditch High Street, failed to do any real damage.
22 July 1938	Terence Stamp was born in Bancroft Road Maternity Hospital (per his autobiography).
23 July 1852	Fraudster Joseph Ady was buried at the Quaker Burial Ground in Whitechapel.
24 July 1852	Poplar Baths in East India Dock Road were opened.
25 July 1884	The first Yiddish Social Journal, *The Poilishe Yidl* (The Little Polish Jew) issued from Commercial Street, E1.
26 July 1654	Anna Trapnell, Poplar 'prophet', was released from imprisonment for witchcraft.
27 July 1913	Police broke up a Federation of Suffragettes meeting at Bromley Hall, Bow Road.
28 July 1873	Wilmot Street 'board school' for 1,600–1,700 pupils opened at Bethnal Green.
29 July 1682	John Balch was granted a licence by Charles II to hold a twice-weekly market at Spitalfields.
30 July 1909	David Lloyd George made a polemical speech in the assembly rooms at Limehouse Town Hall, attacking the House of Lords' opposition to his People's Budget.
31 July 1665	Samuel Pepys was marooned on the Isle of Dogs while awaiting a delayed ferry.

1 August 1921	The Rivoli Theatre opened in Whitechapel.
2 August 1967	The new Blackwall Tunnel opened.
3 August 1937	Steven Berkoff was born in Stepney.
4 August 1806	The opening of the East India Docks took place.
5 August 1583	Sir Humphrey Gilbert, Limehouse navigator and half-brother of Sir Walter Raleigh, landed in Newfoundland and claimed it as England's first overseas colony.
6 August 1937	Actress Barbara Windsor born at the London Hospital.
7 August 1878	The Salvation Army formed at a meeting at 272 Whitechapel Road.
8 August 1921	Frank (later Baron) Chapple was born at St John's Road, Shoreditch: he became first a Communist and then General Secretary of the Electricians' Trade Union.
9 August 2009	Launch of the Cockney Sparrow project at the Peabody Estate, Whitechapel (as a refuge for this endangered bird).
10 August 1885	George 'Gatling Gun' Hilsdon, footballer, born in Bromley-by-Bow.
11 August 1729	The notorious John Gow, pirate, was executed at Wapping Execution Dock.
12 August 1955	Whitechapel gangster Jack 'Spot' Comer stabbed in London.
13 August 1915	George Smith from Bow was hanged: the 'Brides in the Bath' murderer.
14 August 1889	The unloading of the *Lady Armstrong* at West India Dock sparked a strike by thousands of dockers.
15 August 1936	Television gardener Geoff Hamilton was born in Stepney.
16 August 1913	Monty Berman, television/film producer, was born at 25 Whitechapel Road.
17 August 2005	A fund-raiser for the Royal London Hospital was held at the Sonargaon Restaurant in Osborn Street, Whitechapel.
18 August 1978	Doris Waters (Daisy of Bromley-by-Bow comedic duo Gert and Daisy) died.

19 August 1893	Elsie Waters (Gert of Gert and Daisy) was born in Rounton Road, Bromley-by-Bow.
20 August 1912	The death of William Booth of the Salvation Army (formerly the East London Christian Mission).
21 August 1802	West India Dock opened by the Prime Minister, William Pitt.
22 August 1887	Israel Lipski, an umbrella stick salesman living at Batty Street, off Commercial Road, was hanged for the murder of co-tenant Miriam Angel. The crime set off a wave of anti-Semitism in the East End.
23 August 1764	John Wesley preached at Bethnal Green.
24 August 2009	Daniel Radcliffe (Harry Potter) bought a Banksy artwork for £7,000 at a charity auction at Shoreditch House.
25 August 1596	A 'servant of Walter Raleigh' buried at Stepney church (St Dunstan's).
26 August 1892	Emanuel Miller, the renowned psychiatrist, was born at Spitalfields. He worked at the Jewish Hospital in Bethnal Green – the first child guidance clinic in England.
27 August 1802	West India Dock officially opened.
28 August 1921	4,000 East Enders (mainly from Poplar, with a contingent from Bethnal Green, Stepney and Shoreditch) demonstrated at Tower Hill, protesting against unequal rating.
29 August 1877	Wilton's Music Hall destroyed by fire.
30 August 1669	Death of Sir William Rider, owner of 'Kirby's Castle' in Bethnal Green and friend of Samuel Pepys.
31 August 1888	Mary Ann Nichols, allegedly the first Ripper victim, was murdered in Buck's Row, now Durward Street.
1 September 2008	Tower Hamlets introduced a weekly food waste recycling collection to help improve its poor record for recycling.
2 September 1898	Death of Moses Angel, one year after his retirement as headmaster (for 55 years) of the Jews' Free School in Spitalfields.

3 September 1836	Daniel Mendoza, legendary boxer, died at Horseshoe Alley, Petticoat Lane.
4 September 2009	Boris Johnson visited the East London Mosque and London Muslim Centre, Whitechapel.
5 September 1921	Susan Lawrence and other female Poplar councillors were sent to Holloway prison for contempt of court, after defaulting on payment of LCC rates.
6 September 1891	Charles Jamrach, the owner of Jamrach's world famous animal emporium in Ratcliff Highway, died at his Bow home.
7 September 1940	Limehouse docks hit during a bombing raid.
8 September 1589	Naval explorer Sir William Burrough married rich Stepney widow, Lady Jane Wentworth, at St Dunstan's.
9 September 1583	Sir Humphrey Gilbert from Limehouse went down with his ship, the *Squirrel*.
10 September 1940	St Katharine's Dock bombed, destroying all the warehouses.
11 September 1869	The Anti-Vaccination League held a meeting in Limehouse.
12 September 1931	Mahatma Gandhi arrived at Kingsley Hall, Bow, for a twelve-week stay.
13 September 1909	Ted 'Kid' Lewis made his boxing debut at the Judean Social Club, Princes Square: he lost.
14 September 1680	Roger Crab, the Mad Hatter of Bethnal Green, was buried at St Dunstan's.
15 September 1928	Kingsley Hall opened in Powis Road, Bow.
16 September 1889	Dockers returned to work after strike action earned them the 'dockers' tanner' (6*d* per hour).
17 September 1999	Canada Water rail station opened.
18 September 1767	Wapping slave Jonathan Strong appeared in court, and was ruled 'his master's possession'.
19 September 1905	Dr Barnardo, founder of the East End Juvenile Mission (and so much more) died.
20 September 1885	Socialist arrests made at an open air meeting in Dod Street, Limehouse.
21 September 1940	Bethnal Green's first parachute mine caused extensive damage to Allen and Hanbury's factory.

22 September 1729	St Anne's Church, Limehouse, a Hawksmoor church, was consecrated.
23 September 1769	There was rioting at the Dolphin, Bethnal Green, between cutters (silk weavers) and peace officers, with three civilians killed.
24 September 1999	Canary Wharf rail station opened on the Jubilee Line.
25 September 1865	The East London Railway Company took on the ownership of the Thames Tunnel.
26 September 1833	Birth of Charles Bradlaugh at Bethnal Green, politician and advocate of birth control.
27 September 1947	National Savings Campaign procession held in Bethnal Green.
28 September 1946	Helen Shapiro born at Bethnal Green Hospital.
29 September 1957	Footballer Les Sealey born in Bethnal Green.
30 September 1888	Elizabeth Stride murdered in Dutfield's Yard in what was then Berner Street – another murder laid at the door of the Ripper.
1 October 1738	John Wesley preached at St George-in-the-East.
2 October 1732	Goodman's Fields Theatre put on a performance of *Henry IV*.
3 October 1885	First football match for Millwall's 'Rovers'.
4 October 1936	Battle of Cable Street: riots against fascism and the blackshirts.
5 October 1888	The opening of the technical schools in what became the East Wing of the People's Palace, Mile End.
6 October 2006	The first museum of moving art in Britain, the Kinetica, opened in Spitalfields Market.
7 October 1922	Death of Shoreditch music hall star Marie Lloyd.
8 October 1967	Death of Clement Attlee, who was a Stepney Mayor and Limehouse MP before becoming Prime Minister in 1945.
9 October 1769	Hoxton-born Mary Matthews (Drury Lane's lead singer for sixteen years) was married at St Matthew's, Bethnal Green.
10 October 1949	Queues formed to see Dirk Bogarde, in the flesh, at the Odeon, Cambridge Heath Road.
11 October 1884	The Tichborne Claimant, Arthur Orton from Wapping, released from prison.

12 October 1921	Poplar councillors released from prison after being sentenced for their protests against unfair rating.
13 October 1813	Chinese riots at Shadwell.
14 October 1901	A severe fire at Emery and Son, Bow drapers, resulted in two fatalities.
15 October 2008	A Paralympic Talent day was held at Mile End Leisure Centre.
16 October 1756	Sweeney Todd was born at 85 Brick Lane.
17 October 1844	A fire at Blackwall burnt out the Britannia Tavern.
18 October 1996	Blackwall entrepreneurs, the Beckwiths, won a top UK family business award for City Cruises.
19 October 1741	David Garrick made his professional acting debut at Goodman's Fields, playing *Richard III*, billed as 'A Gentleman Who never appeared on any Stage'.
20 October 1968	Death of Bud Flanagan from Whitechapel.
21 October 1872	The Queen of Holland visited Bethnal Green Museum.
22 October 1940	St Mary's station, Whitechapel, hit by a bomb.
23 October 1685	Elizabeth Gaunt of Wapping burnt at the stake for treason.
24 October 1933	The birth of the Kray twins.
25 October 1828	St Katharine's Dock opened.
26 October 1667	Francis Bancroft born at Spitalfields – the founder of Bancroft School which started life on the corner of Bancroft Road, Stepney.
27 October 1916	Robert S. Baker, son of a Whitechapel furrier, was born: actor and scriptwriter, most famous for his scripts for *The Saint*.
28 October 1894	Birth of boxer Ted Lewis at Aldgate.
29 October 1845	Paul Reuter, founder of the news agency, moved to Whitechapel from Germany.

30 October 1825	Final service at the church of St Katharine's before it was demolished to make way for the dock.
31 October 1727	Goodman's Fields Theatre opened in Ayliffe Street, Whitechapel.
1 November 1942	Victoria Park railway station closed.
2 November 1916	George Dorée, the royal weaver, died at London Hospital.
3 November 1831	Murder of the 'Italian boy' by Burkers in Bethnal Green.
4 November 1869	Death of George Peabody, responsible for the first Peabody Buildings which were built in the East End.
5 November 1929	The Duke and Duchess of York opened York Hall in Bethnal Green.
6 November 1897	Annie Toffler fought off two muggers in Cable Street so effectively that she was given a £1 reward for her courage.
7 November 1924	Wolf Mankowitz, prolific writer of fiction and drama, was born in Fashion Street, Spitalfields.
8 November 2002	The Lock Keeper's cottage at Old Ford (the site of the original *Big Breakfast*) was burned down in an arson attack.
9 November 1888	Mary Jane Kelly found murdered in Dorset Street, probably the last of Jack the Ripper's victims.
10 November 1903	Charles Slowe of Rowton House, Whitechapel, was executed for the murder of barmaid Mary Hardwick in the Lord Nelson, Whitechapel Road.
11 November 1928	Limehouse hero Arthur Lovell was killed in an attempt to save a stranger.
12 November 2008	The funeral of Nevio Pellicci, legendary owner of Pellicci's listed 'café' in Bethnal Green.
13 November 1935	George Carey, Archbishop of Canterbury, born in Bow.
14 November 1896	Bud Flanagan born in Hanbury Street, Whitechapel.
15 November 1890	Birth control campaigner Dorothy Thurtle, née Lansbury, was born at St Stephen's Road, Bow.

16 November 1724	The execution of Jack Sheppard, the highwayman from Spitalfields who was renowned for his expertise at escaping from prison.
17 November 1917	The first PDSA opened in Whitechapel.
18 November 1876	Aldgate railway station opened.
19 November 1860	James Mullins was hanged for the murder of Mary Emsley at her Grove Road home in Mile End.
20 November 1862	Lewis Lyons, the influential figure in London's Jewish tailoring trade unions, was born in Whitechapel.
21 November 1853	Nathaniel Mobbs of Whitechapel was hanged for the murder of his wife.
22 November 1996	Bow-born celebrity photographer, Terence Donovan, hanged himself.
23 November 1916	Death of Charles Booth, the social reformer who wrote in depth about the poverty in Tower Hamlets.
24 November 1892	Fire broke out at Hermitage Wharf, High Street, Wapping, and needed over 200 men to bring it under control.
25 November 1912	A Suffragettes' torch-lit rally took place outside Bow Church on the eve of polling day.
26 November 1869	North Street, Stepney, changed its name to Fairclough Street.
27 November 1855	HMS *Julia* launched at Limehouse by Fletcher and Fearnall.
28 November 1937	Rose Cohen, the East End founder member of the British Communist party, executed as an enemy of the state.
29 November 1936	Oswald Mosley's first open-air meeting at Poplar – Newby Place.
30 November 1869	The Prince of Wales attended Wilton's Music Hall.
1 December 1930	Matt Monro born in Shoreditch.
2 December 1884	Dr Treves from the London Hospital 'exhibited' Joseph Merrick, the Elephant Man, to the Pathological Society of London.

3 December 1611	Ratcliff sea captain Thomas Best was appointed Chief Commander of the East India Company's tenth fleet.
4 December 1920	The Duke of York unveiled the Bromley Central Ward War Memorial in Bromley-by-Bow.
5 December 1759	The main block of the London Hospital was completed.
6 December 1769	Two weavers were hanged in front of the Salmon and Ball pub in Bethnal Green.
7 December 1869	Wapping rail station opened.
8 December 1760	John Tune executed at Wapping's Execution Dock for piracy.
9 December 1858	Foundation stone laid for Wilton's Music Hall.
10 December 1893	Birth of Alfred Drake at Mile End, recipient of a posthumous VC.

11 December 1662	John Seller, who sold maps from premises at Wapping Old Stairs, tried for high treason.
12 December 1821	Death of Phoebe Hessel, the Stepney Amazon.
13 December 1998	Shoreditch-educated Baron Lew Grade, the entertainment mogul, died.
14 December 1870	Nathaniel Heckford died of overwork at just 29 after founding the East London Children's Hospital. Note: some sources give 1871.
15 December 1812	Destined to become the proprietor of the *Sunday Times*, Joseph Levy was born at Whitechapel.

16 December 1872   George Fredericks took over Wilton's Music Hall.

17 December 1830   The last two men to be executed at Execution Dock, Wapping, were hanged for murder and mutiny.

18 December 1887   The funeral of Bow's Alfred Linnell at Bow cemetery attracted a huge turn-out. He had been trampled to death by a police horse on Bloody Sunday.

19 December 1606   Three ships set out from Blackwall Stairs for Virgina, captained by John Smith.

20 December 1980   Footballer Ashley Cole born in Stepney.

21 December 1875   Henry Wainwright hanged at Newgate for the murder of his mistress at his Whitechapel warehouse.

22 December 2007   The East London underground line closed.

23 December 1996   Ronnie Scott, Wapping-born jazz supremo, died.

24 December 1608   William Davison, diplomat and secretary to Queen Elizabeth I, was buried at St Dunstan's, near his home.

25 December 1731   Jacob Bourdillon became minister of L'Eglise de l'Artillerie, Spitalfields.

26 December 1878   Successful artiste, Ada Reeve from Stepney, made her theatrical debut in *Red Riding Hood* at the Mile End Pavilion, age 4.

27 December 1813   Lord Castlereagh had to dismount at Aldgate on his way to Harwich due to the icy yellow fog.

28 December 1825   The death of John Thomas Serres, painter of 'The Thames at Limehouse'.

29 December 1860   The first iron-clad warship, the *Warrior*, launched at Blackwall.

30 December 1906   Death of Baroness Burdett-Coutts, the philanthropist who did so much for East Enders.

31 December 1811   John Williams – main suspect in the Ratcliff Highway Murders – was buried at the crossroads of Cannon Street Road and Back Lane with a stake through his heart (the practice with suicides).

ACKNOWLEDGMENTS

Ahuge list of people have helped with this book, which covers such a wide range of subjects, albeit within a confined area of London. I have realised, since writing local history, that there is always an expert out there somewhere – and most are more than willing to help! As far as this book is concerned, these have been my main sources of assistance: Christopher Lloyd and Malcolm Barr-Hamilton at Tower Hamlets Local History Library and Archives, Dorothy Gorsuch at the Coopers Company and Coborn School, Jonathan Evans and Shannon Gillespie at the Royal London Hospital, Turia Tellwright at the British Horseracing Authority, Mhairi Ellis at St Botolph-without-Bishopsgate, Paul Smith at Thomas Cook Company Archives, Fiona Cormack at the Museum of London, Joseph Payne at the Royal Mint, Tony Drake at the Bluebell Railway Museum, Louise Mead at Queen Mary (University of London), Paul S. Marshall (author), Caroline Warhurst at the London Transport Museum, John Graves at the National Maritime Museum, Inge Schoups at the Stad Antwerpen, Canon Michael Ainsworth at St George-in-the-East, Maurice Bitton at Bevis Marks Synagogue and Andrew Wyatt at the Tate Gallery.

I would also like to acknowledge the assistance of www.clipart. com, Toby Williams (pp. iv, 21, 114, 129, 144) and Heather Lenzam (p. 140) for their contributions to the illustrations used. Others are out-of-copyright illustrations from nineteenth-century issues of *Punch* magazine.

There are at least two sources (usually three) for every snippet within these pages, often a combination of books, newspapers (*East London Advertiser, East London Observer, The Times, Penny Illustrated, The Graphic, Illustrated London News, East London Life*) and the internet. Where the latter is concerned, the most reliable sources when it comes to verifying material have proved to be:

www.oxforddnb.com
www.portcities.org.uk
www.british-history.ac.uk
www.eastlondonhistory.com
www.mernick.org.uk

www.capitalpunishmentuk.org
www.canarywharf.com
www.stgite.org.uk
www.subbrit.org.uk
www.exploringeastlondon.co.uk

Other titles published by The History Press

The Little Book of London
David Long
978-07509-4800-5

A funny, fast-paced, fact-packed compendium of the sort of frivolous, fantastic or simply strange information which no-one should be without. Literally hundreds of wacky facts about the world's greatest city make this required reading for locals and visitors alike.

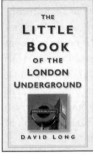

The Little Book of the London Underground
David Long
978-07524-5225-8

With a history stretching back nearly 150 years, the world's oldest underground railway might seem familiar, but actually, how well do you know it? This book will tell you everything you need to know – and plenty more your probably don't!

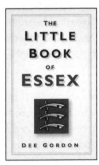

The Little Book of Essex
Dee Gordon
978-07509-5127-2

Packed full of entertaining, bite-sized pieces of trivia, be amused and amazed at the stories and history of Essex's landscape, towns, villages, heritage, buildings and, above all, its people.

Visit our website and discover thousands of other History Press books.

www.thehistorypress.co.uk